I Am the Exception

I Am the Exception

*A Mother's Story of Rape Conception
and the Grace of God*

Anna Richey

CONTRA MUNDUM | PRO MUNDO

Copyright © 2015 by Anna Richey

All rights reserved. No portion of this book may be reproduced, stored in a retrieval system, or transmitted in any form or by any means—electronic, mechanical, photocopy, recording, or otherwise—except for brief quotations in reviews or articles, without the prior written consent of The New Clapham Press.

The New Clapham Press
P.O. Box 68
Noble, OK 73068
www.newclaphampress.com

The mission of The New Clapham Press is to bring the Gospel of the Lord Jesus Christ into conflict with the evils of our age, through the publication of print and electronic media. We believe the Gospel is the answer to sin, and we desire to see all men repent and follow the Lord Jesus Christ. As such, we are against the world, for the world.

ISBN-13: 978-1-943807-01-7
ISBN-10: 1-943807-01-9

1. Biography & Autobiography / Personal Memoirs
2. Biography & Autobiography / Religious
3. Religion / Christian Life / Inspirational

First Edition: July 2015
10 9 8 7 6 5 4 3 2 1

*To my family and friends who believed and supported me,
and the abolitionists who encouraged me to write my story.*

Foreword

By Don Cooper

I first met Anna Richey at an abolitionist conference in Norman, Oklahoma. In the auditorium of a small church building, Anna shared her story with about 100 other abolitionists. When she was finished speaking, there wasn't a dry eye in the room. Anna hardly knew anyone there. She had agreed to speak at the request of fellow abolitionists who knew that her story needed to be heard. Anna apologized for not being a polished speaker, which never crossed our minds as we listened to her story. She spoke not as a professional orator entertaining the audience, but rather as a daughter, a woman, and a mother, who had been tried by fire and sustained by God.

For many years prior to this time, I participated in pro-life activism and events. I devoted a great deal of time and energy to the fight for the unborn. Like most pro-life individuals, I voted for pro-life candidates and got behind pro-life legislation. But it was not until I heard Anna's story that I began to feel the weight of the sin of compromise that filled so much of my pro-life activism.

During my years as a pro-life activist, I had a small number of friends who were adamantly opposed to abortion like I was, but they were different. They viewed compromising tactics as wrong. In fact, I used to argue with them about this. I would tell them that they were being fools. That they were wasting their votes. That they didn't understand how we would incrementally end abortion by "taking what we can get now."

My friends were patient with me and stood their ground. As I was continually challenged on these compromising tactics that I fully supported, I began to see the possible harm and wrong in what I was doing. Eventually, God was able to penetrate my hard heart, and the seed that my abolitionist friends had planted and cultivated began to grow.

It became clear to me that if we are called to speak truth to the world regarding the plight of the unborn, that we could not compromise by endorsing abortion in cases of rape. *If we are supposed to be the ones proclaiming that all human beings are made in the image of God and that all have right to life, how can we say that babies conceived in rape can be killed?* Is this not a gross sin at worst, and a needlessly confusing message at best?

And then I began to consider what Jesus said in Matthew 25—that whatever we did for the "least of these," we did for Him. And that whatever we did not do for the least of these, we did not do for Him. If this is true, are we not turning our backs on the "least of these" when we endorse a political candidate or legislation that permits orphans to be dismembered by a paid killer?

Are there any circumstances in which it would be justified in God's eyes to turn our backs on His Son, and Him before the world? Is there a cause good enough to excuse such an act? Does Scripture anywhere teach that "the end justifies the means?"

Who are the "least of these" in our culture? Could the "least of these" be poor people who are so poor that they have no clothes on their backs? Could they be the defenseless who are so weak or small that others who are stronger and larger can take advantage of them? Could they be those who are so alone that their own parents have abandoned them?

Consider the young girl who is a victim of repeated rape by her stepfather. Is this young girl not one of the "least of these," and are we not to care for her? Consider a child conceived in such a circumstance. This child is a baby made in the image of God whose father is a criminal of the worst sort. And yet, the "help" our culture offers is abortion—to simply murder the innocent child. And in recommending this "help," even the "champions" for the plight of the young girl are in agreement with our godless culture.

Imagine if you were this baby and all the "help" that was being offered was advice that you should be murdered by dismemberment and your body pitched in the trash. Would you not desire rescue?! Is this little baby not qualified more than anyone else to be the "least of these?"

When the evil of child rape occurs, and it results in a child being conceived, we have not one, but two victims to care for. And both victims are the "least of these." Who will care for these victims as God desires, if not God's own people? We must do so without compromise, without shame, and without reservation.

When we show support of any kind for ideas and actions that permit the murder of these rape-conceived babies, we are turning our backs on the "least of these." We are also turning our backs on Christ Himself, according to His own words.

When we consider it good or permissible to endorse a strategy that tells our culture that a legitimate way to deal with the horrible crime of rape is to murder the most innocent victim of that vicious act, we are guilty of the worst crime of all. We are saying it is permissible to murder Christ Himself. In fact, we are guilty if we do not actively oppose such an anti-Christian idea, and not merely abstain from supporting it.

When we tell mothers, either in a tacit or overt manner, that we think that to murder their own offspring, based on their circumstances of conception, is a "choice" they sometimes need, we are defiling the very motherhood that led to the birth of our own Savior.

Now, I know that most pro-life people do not believe that abortion ought to be permitted in cases of rape or incest, or in any other condition. But we have been deceived if we think that our personal opinions are all that matter, and that our actions have no significant effect on what the world sees and hears.

Our actions speak louder than words. And for the last 42 years, the movement that should primarily be teaching the culture that abortion is murder and that it ought to be immediately abolished, is instead preaching a message—through lobbying, political action, sermons, and countless financial donations—that support the murder of babies conceived in rape and incest.

Is it any wonder that the culture believes there are difficult circumstances that justify abortion, especially rape and incest? Is it any wonder that abortion on-demand is further solidified instead of undone?

But all these arguments pale in comparison to the real story we read here. The story of a real little girl, not unlike any little girl you know or have known. A girl who is no different than your own daughter. The same as your sister. The same as your best friend. No different than the little girl your mother was. No different than the little girl your wife was. Perhaps no different than you.

What was the message Anna should have heard when she was faced with her trials? What was the message the pro-life movement was preaching while her stepfather continually raped her? What were the actions of the churches in America when Anna's stepfather forced an abortion upon her so he could continue his appalling act? Was not the pro-life movement complicit in the continued abuse of this little child? When the pro-life movement took action to uphold the rape-incest exception, were they not aiding and abetting Anna's rapist?

Did not abortion enable Anna's stepfather to continue his hidden evil act? And did not our culture, including the pro-life movement, agree that this is surely that exception which justifies abortion?

As Christians, when we side with pragmatism that is counter to God's word, we effectively rewrite history. We act as if Moses took Pharaoh's offer to only let some of the people go for a short time. We tell a version of the account of Josiah tearing down some of the high places so as to wean the children of Israel from burning incense to false gods. We tell a story of Daniel, who decided he would stop praying to the Lord of the universe for a season in order to persuade the king of Babylon. We rewrite the acts of the Apostles as calling the people to gradually curb their routine practices of idolatry instead of repenting immediately.

When we side with the idea that exceptions which justify abortion are in any way tolerable, we have sided with the pedophile who uses abortion to perpetually carry on his act in the dark. When we agree, even if through a putatively temporary agreement, to link arms with political pragmatism in opposition to the Spirit of the Prophets of old, *we are agreeing instead with the abortionist who makes money off the blood of innocent children.*

How is it possible that God's people, even for a fraction of a second, could trade the message of His redeeming power for a message of demonic destruction? Anna expresses so innocently and eloquently how even while she was in a living Hell, God provided a sliver of Heaven to help her endure. Why do we deny this message and the power of God?

And how can we, born again believers in the Son of Man, even entertain the idea of siding with the pro-abortion activist who unabashedly claims we need abortion in order to care for rape victims? As I once heard Anna say so directly, "They [abortion advocates] no longer speak for us [rape victims]." God has spoken for the fatherless and oppressed, and we will stand by what He says.

As I read Anna's narrative, I was reminded of the words of slavery abolitionist William Lloyd Garrison regarding the narrative of a victim of slavery. The evil of his time was just like abortion, in that it was the result of denying the image of God in man. Human beings where being treated like animals to be worked to death, and property to be bought and sold at auction. In that day, many "good" people tolerated this defilement of God's image. Garrison wrote concerning the story of Frederick Douglas, and I apply his words to Anna's narrative:

> He who can peruse it without a tearful eye, a heaving breast, an afflicted spirit—without being filled with an unutterable abhorrence of [abortion] slavery, and all its abettors, and animated with a determination to seek the immediate overthrow of that execrable system—without trembling for the fate of this country in the hands of a righteous God, who is ever on the side of the oppressed, and whose arm is not shortened that it cannot save—must have a flinty heart, and be qualified to act the part of a [murderer of children in the womb] trafficker in slaves and souls of men.

I cannot remember if there was loud applause or utter silence after we heard Anna's story in that small building in Norman. I do recall my heart feeling like it weighed a thousand pounds. I do recall that while everyone in that room was filled with an inexpressible sorrow for the sufferings endured by this young lady, we were also filled with an unspeakable joy in the power of God to overcome. She stood before us that day, beaten but not broken, a victim of the worst crimes imaginable, but an abolitionist of the "solution" our culture offers to her plight. A bold voice for truth, as one who lived through the fire of Nebuchadnezzar's oven, she is a New Creation in Christ, bringing the world a message of inspiration, hope, truth, and love.

There were no words for the weight of that moment. A million thoughts went through my mind, but one stood out prominently in that moment. The Holy Spirit was speaking succinctly to me. I needed to apologize to Anna and her daughter Josey. I needed to apologize for all the years I was complicit in promoting a pro-life agenda that sacrificed these girls, and others like them, to Moloch. I needed to ask their forgiveness for aiding her attacker and abandoning her to pragmatism.

Even if my intentions were good when I helped campaign for pro-life candidates, it did not change the fact that I was promoting the idea that we could compromise the lives of these little ones. I had been deluded in believing that I was pursuing "good works," but I now realized that the end never justifies the means. I was wrong. Very wrong. And it wasn't enough that I change direction and stop endorsing compromisers. The least I could do was to apologize to those before me who had been hurt. The least I could do was to boldly stand in the gap for Anna and those like her.

Ultimately, we see in Anna's story that God does not operate in the linear way we often think He ought. The Lord can take even the greatest tragedies and turn them to good in our lives if we are faithful to Him and His word. The greatest example of this is the redemption and reconciliation He has brought to pass through the crucifixion of His Son, and His resurrection from the dead.

We see also that the Lord is able to accomplish the impossible through His people, if we remain faithful to his precepts and commandments. How can God bring about good through the most heinous crimes against an innocent child? How can God bring redemption to a little girl who is abandoned by her father and by most of the world? How can a young woman forgive her abusers and let go of bitterness? Read, and you will see how God did this in Anna. With man it is impossible, but with God it is possible. *The power of God is real and has no limits.*

How can we abolish human abortion—a practice entrenched in our culture, responsible for the murder of more innocent children than any other act devised by the devil? We do this by uncompromisingly and unashamedly opposing the evil God's way, not man's way.

How did abortion grow to the scale it is today? *Through compromise,* in large part. Abortion thrives on a compromising Spirit. And how can we abolish it tomorrow? Only by an uncompromising Spirit.

If we learn anything from Anna's story, it is this: *God calls us to promote redemption, not destruction.* We see this throughout Anna's story. God is the giver of life. God is the redeemer. God is in the business of accomplishing the impossible and taking us through the trials we never thought it possible to endure. And He not only delivers us from our trials, but He gives us joy and peace in their midst!

God would never have us proclaim any other message. We proclaim redemption in Christ always and everywhere. We call to the world to repent and turn to the One who loves the fatherless, the widow, the oppressed and the helpless. We should never in any way promote destruction in place of God's redeeming power.

If you are one of those who, like me, thought the way to end abortion was a path of compromise that, even for a moment, abandons the little ones like Anna and her children—then repent now. No longer compromise with Pharaoh. No longer bow your knee to Nebuchadnezzar. No longer believe the devil's lie that God prefers pragmatism to His Word. Oppose the compromising ideas, strategies and tactics that deny justice for the fatherless and the oppressed. For then we will truly and actively be loving the millions of little children, like Anna, her daughter Josey, and her unborn child who did not survive the evil of our age.

ANNA RICHEY

When we love as God has called us to love, when we serve as God has called us to serve, and when we fight as God has called us to fight, we can, by the power of God, abolish human abortion.

— 1 —

Growing up, some children wish for special families—families that make them stand out from the crowd. Perhaps they are rich and powerful. Maybe they are musical or inventive. Other children are blessed with loving parents who provide wonderful—although never perfect—homes, and they realize it. They are thankful for what they have and are generally happy. Still others wish for families that are "normal"—families where mom and dad are a little less embarrassing. Maybe their parents try too hard to be "cool." Perhaps they have a somewhat odd sense of fashion. Maybe they are even a bit eccentric.

Some of us, though, grow up wishing that our family could be "safe." A place where we can go to be loved, not hurt. A home that we don't have to fear.

Many children from this last category often daydream about being orphans. They believe that a lack of a family must be better than what they face at home.

But God has given each of us the desire to be loved and accepted. That is why you find so many children from unsafe, unhappy homes running away, joining gangs, or being promiscuous. Those children want so badly to be loved and accepted. But how, if you are born into darkness, can you ever know to search for the sun? Such children are scared and confused. Because of their situation at home, they do not know what real love looks like.

Scared, confused, searching children will reach out to anyone who shows them any kind of care or concern. They often don't realize that they are being used. If they do realize it, they do not see why it is wrong. They have grown to believe that they deserve to be treated in this way. These children have no idea of their worth or potential. They have never known the very things that most people take for granted in their own lives.

My home was almost normal once. My father was an alcoholic, but he was a happy drunk. Not once in my memory did he yell or get violent when he drank. He laughed at everything. The biggest problem was that he drank away his paychecks, and had a horrible habit of driving while under the influence. My memories of him generally consisted of laughter and mirth. He was a logger in the Uinta Mountains, outside

Manila, Utah. I remember him being a hard worker, even though he suffered from severe pain most of the time. Before I was born, my father was badly injured when he was crushed by several hefty logs in a truck loading accident at work. He suffered a broken pelvis and several breaks in his back, but my father was blessed to be alive.

My mom was a hard worker who had always just wanted a family to love and care for. She married my dad not long after high school, and became a mother when she had me at the age of 23. She had not had the opportunity to attend college, and took nearly any job she could get in order to help make ends meet. Usually her jobs consisted of cooking, waitressing, and housekeeping. She always tried to put her husband first—at least until she thought doing so would be dangerous for her children.

My father had six children—three from a previous marriage and three from my mom. I had two older brothers and an older sister. I don't remember much about my older siblings from when I was young, mostly just vague images and feelings that hang upon the walls of my mind like blurry photographs. In one, we are playing tag in the woods. In another, we try to catch fish in the creek with our bare hands. These memories are few and spread far apart, but they are happy.

I was the oldest of my mom's children, followed by my younger brother and then my baby sister. We lived in Manila, a little town of about 3,000 residents, perched in the mountains near the Flaming Gorge in Utah. My mom tried to make things work with my dad, but she was worried about what his drinking was doing to our family. Although I was never told the reason for the final break, there came a point at which she could take no more. She found a job as a cook at a resort about 30 miles from town, took her three kids, and fled.

Mom stayed near home for a while, hoping that my dad would decide that he loved his family more than the booze. Unfortunately, that didn't happen. After a time, she met another man, the proverbial "tall, dark, and handsome" kind. He seemed to be a hard worker who loved spending time with her and her children. As a bonus, he didn't drink. Instead, he took us white water rafting and made her dinner. He bought her roses and told her how wonderful she was.

They married, and for a while, life seemed wonderful. It has been my experience that all children want a loving mom and dad. We had a "normal" family again. It was then, as I began to curl up into this corner of pseudo-safety, that the nightmare began. The truth about my new father was soon revealed. It was in the darkness that he came for me, and it was in darkness that he was unmasked. I developed two lives. One the world saw—the other I had only in my heart and in my head. The little girl the world saw was quiet, nervous around others, and cried easily. The one in my heart was a raging mess. She screamed, yelled, broke things, and was exceedingly violent.

While I don't remember a great deal of my childhood, things start to become clearer around 1990. We lived in Brigham City, Utah, and I was in the third grade. The first book I remember from that year was "The Big Friendly Giant." I remember sitting in class and thinking how wonderful it would be to be kidnapped by a friendly giant and taken away to live in his cave. That was where my love of books began. I discovered that I could escape to whatever world I wanted, where no one could hurt me.

I fled into a world of fantasy and fiction. I didn't really care what the book was about, as long as it wasn't real. Eventually, I even began writing my own stories. Looking back on them now, I realize those stories were horrible, and not because they were poorly written. All the main characters in my books were female, usually young orphans. There was nearly always a man as the antagonist, and she would dispatch him in cruel, gruesome, and gory ways. She was strong, though, and she always won. No one could hurt her.

My mom wondered what had happened to her happy little girl, and I remember her asking me about it. But my stepfather had told me that if anyone ever discovered our dark swelling secret, then my mom would go to jail, and my siblings and I would be split up and put into foster homes where all sorts of horrible things would happen. Like most children, I believed what I was told. I told my mom that I missed my real dad and my brothers and sister, and that I didn't like my new school. She spent some extra time with me trying to talk to me about how I would grow to like my new school and make new friends. I learned to hide things from my mom better than I had before. I couldn't risk her finding out. I hid within the prison I hated.

I remember being in the same school for the fourth grade, and after a particularly rough night, sitting by the fence in the playground crying. I remember one of my classmates walking over to my teacher and asking what was wrong with me. I remember my teacher telling her not to mind me because I was always crying—just looking for attention. She couldn't have been standing more than 20 feet from me, and I heard every word. That was when I learned that I should never cry.

By the time I was in the fifth grade, I had made two relatively close friends. That is as close as I dared to let anyone get. They never came to my house for the night, but eventually I was allowed a sleepover at one of their houses. I remember marveling at her family and how "normal" they were. I remember being so very, very jealous. That night, after her parents were asleep, we played the classic "truth or dare" sleepover game. My friend asked me if I was a virgin, fully expecting me to start blushing and to say "Yes! Of course." What a simple, innocent question for a young girl, yet here I was with my innocence tarnished. How could I answer? I lied to her and never went back to her house.

I discovered that I could never have friendships like the ones I had read and fantasized about. I could never be that open or honest with anyone. I would always have a secret that would set me apart from everyone around me. At times, the loneliness seemed unbearable. I wanted so badly to have someone I could trust, someone to confide in. My secret was so very heavy, too heavy for my small and damaged frame. How could I bear it alone?

That same year, I was introduced to God for the first time. There was a church down the street from our house, and we were invited. We went a few times, and I was even allowed to go to Vacation Bible School and then church camp. I adored every minute of it. The people all seemed so nice, so open, and so helpful. And Jesus! Oh, Jesus sounded like the answer to everything! When they gave the altar call after church camp, I came forward and vowed to give my life to Him, to accept Him as my Savior. Oh, how I needed a Savior, and I wanted Him to be my Savior more than anything!

I returned home from camp so full of hope! Surely, if Jesus didn't just make my stepfather go away, then He would at least make him into a real dad just like the ones my friends had! Finally, I would have that normal family I had been dreaming about! We would laugh and read the Bible and have picnics in the park!

Oh, how wonderful life would be now that Jesus was in charge!

But He didn't do anything. Nothing had changed at all. Only now, I had no hope of ever escaping. I thought of running away, but then what would happen to my little sister? Would he hurt her? Or my brother? What about my mom? What would she do? I could handle whatever he did to me. I would make myself handle it. But I could not accept knowing that he had hurt someone else in my family because of my actions.

Not long after this bleak realization, I remember being in the shower before school. I started crying, and I couldn't stop. I was crying so hard that my brother came to the door, wanting to know if I was alright. I knew I needed to stop, to be strong again, but I just couldn't. Why wasn't I good enough for Jesus? They said that He loved all the little children, but they lied. He didn't love me. I was completely alone. I now knew there was a God. My experience at the church had taught me that, but He didn't care about me. I knew Him, but I hated Him.

After the school year ended, we moved again, this time to Vernal, Utah. I was happy with the move. My mom's family lived in Vernal. I had grandparents, an aunt, an uncle, and cousins. I couldn't wait to see them. My stepfather's family lived there as well, but I didn't know them. We moved in with his parents when we first got to Vernal, while my mom found a job and looked for a new home for us. It wasn't bad there. The abuse didn't stop, but with so many people around, it did at least slow down.

Eventually, my mom did find a job, and we had a new home at one of the trailer parks on the outskirts of town. I was enrolled into the middle school where I would be surrounded by hundreds of other kids. My plan was to avoid everyone and focus on my grades, so I could get a good job someday and be able to escape. I wanted a new life so badly.

I did end up making a small group of friends, despite my determination not to. We shared our love of movies, books, and music. We had sleepovers and shared secrets as all girls do—except for mine. To this day, I am so very grateful that God sent those girls to stand by me through the hardest times of my life.

I became pregnant for the first time when I was 12. At first, I was violently ill for the first part of the morning. I felt strange. Parts of me were growing that hadn't before, and everything felt sensitive. I didn't know what to do! I believed that I would lose my family if anyone found out, and that I would be thrown into foster care or some kind of institution for what they would surely call "girls like me."

The only thing I could think to do was tell my stepfather. As an adult, he would know what to do. That one decision would be the absolute worst of my life; the one thing I regret. He was furious with me. My mom was gone to work, and he left me in charge of my siblings while he drove into town. A little while later, he returned. He sent my siblings down the street to the park to play. Once they were gone, he pulled a little box out of a shopping bag, poured me a glass of water, and gave me two of the pills that were in the box.

After I had swallowed them, he punched me in the stomach, slapped me, and told me as I stood there stinging that if I told anyone, there would be serious trouble. At the time, I couldn't understand why he hit me. I wasn't going to tell anyone, that's why I had told *him*. He left again, and I went to my room to lay down. I wasn't feeling well at that point. My stomach was cramping, and I ached all over. I lay there and cried until I fell asleep. A few hours later, the cramping got worse. I went to find someone, but I found a note on the table saying that mom was working late, and my stepfather had taken the other kids to visit his family.

By the next morning, I was feverish, and I could hardly stand because the pain was so severe. My mom called the school to tell them I wouldn't be in, and then she went to work. By the time she got home, I was no longer pregnant. However, I was throwing up, which just confirmed to her that I had a stomach virus and needed to stay in bed and rest.

I had become pretty good at hiding things at this point. So I did with this new and separate pain what I did with all my secret agonies—I tucked it away. I wouldn't even speak of the child I had lost until years later. I doubled my efforts in school and worked harder at everything than ever before. I retreated into my books and my music. I watched every movie I could get my hands on. Anything so I wouldn't have to think. Life moved on, and the abuse continued.

— 2 —

Early in the spring of 1995, I noticed that there were changes happening in my body again. At first, I hoped that it was just the normal changes that I saw the other girls in my school going through. But then I noticed that I had missed my period. Twice. I didn't know what to do. I remembered what had happened last time, and there was no way I could let that happen again. I couldn't tell my mom or anyone else, or I would lose my family. What could I do?

I hid it. I pretended that nothing was wrong and that everything was normal. But all the while, I was searching for someone I could tell, someone who could help me. But it all came back to protecting my family. Regardless of how much I wanted to say something, I believed I would still lose my family in the end.

The months passed, and the pregnancy progressed. March came, and I was running out of time. My body was changing rapidly now. I had started the year at around 75 pounds and was flat as a board. By the end of March, I was approaching 90 pounds and had suddenly started developing breasts and hips. I had also started growing a slight baby bump. I knew I couldn't hide my baby much longer. I had to find someone to tell, and fast.

Although I didn't know it when I woke up that morning, April 1, 1995 was a day that would change my life forever. My stepfather had gone to work, and my mom had called me into the dining room. She told me she wanted to do my nails, which wasn't surprising to me. My Aunt Marsha had been teaching her how to apply acrylic nails using a certain kind of paste and chemical. I didn't know how it worked. I only knew that my mom had been using my sister and me to practice on. I didn't mind, as it gave me a chance to spend some quality time with her. She worked so much that we kids didn't get as much time with her as we would have liked.

Something was different this time. She appeared somehow nervous as she began. I remember her hands shaking ever so slightly as she opened the jars so she could make the paste she would use to form the nails. As she got started, she first asked me about school, how I was enjoying my classes, and told me how proud of me she was for the good grades I making. I could tell there was something else on her mind; she wouldn't look me in the eye. As she stroked my right thumbnail with her little brush, I asked her what was wrong.

She told me that she had noticed some changes in me and had also noticed that I had not asked her to buy me any feminine products in a few months. Then she took a deep, unsteady breath and asked me if I was pregnant. This was my chance. Regardless of what happened next, I had to tell her the truth. My child's life depended on it.

I said "Yes."

At this point, her hands were trembling so badly that my freshly painted thumbnail had a definite sideways angle. She put down the brush and asked me who the father was. I told her and watched as all the blood drained from her face. I was terrified that she was going to pass out. I jumped up and ran over to her, hoping to catch her if she started to fall. Somehow, she managed to stay upright. She whispered that I needed to go get my brother and sister and meet her at the car.

When I returned, she appeared to have herself a little more under control. She still looked pale, and her hands were still shaking. I remember the sound of the car doors slamming shut after we all piled into her little car, and my little sister complaining because she was going to miss a play date with the little girl who lived down the street. Shock and fear started to settle into my heart as I realized what I had done. I had told the secret. What would happen now? Were we running away?

My mom was silent as we drove, but every now and again I would sneak a glance at her as she wiped tear after tear off of her cheeks. Sorrow crept in with the terrible fear and shock that moved inside my chest. I had hurt my mom. My body was shaking as I tried to crawl deeper into my seat so I could hide. Maybe if I could make myself small enough, I would disappear, and it would all be over.

I closed my eyes and willed that the words I had finally let live would crawl back into my head and die. Why, oh why, couldn't I keep my big mouth shut?!

I opened my eyes when I felt the car stop. We were at the grocery store. Mom told the three of us to wait in the car, she would be right back. She went in and came back out just a few moments later with the handles of a small plastic bag poking out of the purse gripped between her fingers.

She drove us to the other side of town, where my Aunt Marsha lived. My brother and sister were pleased; they jumped out of the car and ran to find my cousins. I hadn't realized I was crying until I felt my mom reach over and wipe the tears from my face. She told me it was going to be alright. I didn't believe her; had I ever been alright? She grabbed my hand and held it for a moment before taking a deep breath and stepping out of the car. I couldn't get my legs to cooperate, so I stayed right where I was.

I watched my mom walk up to the house, where my aunt met her at the door. Before going inside, my mom turned back and motioned for me to follow her. In a haze, I obeyed. I could hear my heart pounding as I walked into the house. I could see my mom sitting at the table in the kitchen, and I headed in there. Marsha brought over a cup of coffee for herself and my mom and sat down. We all just sat there in silence for a moment.

Finally, my mom reached down into her purse and handed me the little sack she had brought from the grocery store. She told me to take it into the bathroom and follow the directions on the box. She said she had to talk to my aunt, and then she would be right in. I took the bag and did as I was told.

I did not trust my legs as I made my way down the hall into the bathroom. I had already seen and felt what those pills can do to a person. Is that what my mom had gotten for me? Was I supposed to take those again? I wouldn't do it, I decided. I would flush them down the toilet, and then when no one was looking, I would run. I had no idea where I would go, but I would never do that again. I refused to take part in killing another one of my children.

I went into the bathroom and sat down on the edge of the tub. I pulled the box from the plastic bag, and my heart leapt up into my throat. It wasn't pills! It was a pregnancy test! For a moment, I just sat there staring at the little box in my hand. My mind was in such a fog that I had to read the directions three times before the words finally sank in.

I was sitting back on the edge of the tub, awaiting the results of the test, when I heard the crash and the screaming from the kitchen. I jumped up and ran to my mom as fast as I could. When I reached the door to the kitchen, I saw my mom sitting at the table crying. My aunt had thrown her coffee mug across the room and punched the steel door that led to the back porch. I could see where the metal had dented, and she was cradling her hand. Surely, she had broken something.

I must have made some kind of sound because they both turned to look at me. My aunt ran over and hugged me. She kept telling me the same thing that my mom had said, that I was going to be alright. She stroked my hair and just repeated over and over, "It's going to be okay, Honey. It's going to be okay." After a moment, I felt my mom hugging me too. We all just stood there with my mom and aunt crying for several minutes. It was then that it started to sink in that maybe, just maybe, it really would be alright.

We finally broke apart, and my aunt went to clean up the mess she had made. Mom took my hand, and we went back down the hall to see the results of the test. On our way, she told me that they had already called the police, and my stepfather would be arrested as soon as he returned to the house from work. We went into the bathroom, and my mom picked up the little stick from where I had left it on the counter. Looking at the little window on the test, she blinked a few times and then asked me to hand her the box. I did and watched her eyes dart back and forth between the two objects. When she looked back at me, she had tears in her eyes again.

"You are pregnant, Honey" she told me. "You are going to have a baby." Now, I had already known that. I had known that for months, actually. But for some reason, hearing my mom say the words made it real for me. I started to feel dizzy, and I felt the room start to spin. With those few words, my mom had told me so much. My baby wasn't going to die! My mom said I was going to have a baby. And so I was!

The police came to my aunt's house not long after. My mom said it was normal, and that I should tell them the truth about what had happened. I was also told that I would be taken to the hospital first, where they would run some tests on me to make sure that my baby and I were okay. I was told that my little sister would also have to be tested "just to see."

I was confused—so very, very confused. I had been told for years that I wasn't to tell anyone what had happened, especially someone with any kind of authority! If I did, I would lose my family. Now my mom wanted me to tell everything? I could feel a knot of panic forming in my stomach. I couldn't do this! If I could just run away, then my family could stay together, and my baby would be safe, too! But where would I go? I couldn't take care of a child alone. I couldn't even take care of myself!

My internal argument lasted through the majority of the hospital tests that they put us through. When they had finished with us, the doctor spoke to all of us, including the police officer who had driven us there. He informed us that I was indeed pregnant. He also informed us that my little sister had been molested as well. I started crying. All I had done to try to protect her had been for nothing. *He had hurt her anyway!*

The doctor gave some papers to the police officer, and I assumed they were the results of the tests that had been given to us. I really didn't care at the time. I had other things that concerned me far more. After being told that my little sister had been molested as well, my mom broke. She just sat there, crying, and staring off into space. It was like she wasn't even in the same room as the rest of us. Even now, I can only imagine what was running through her mind.

When the doctor had finished speaking with the officer, he asked if he could speak to my mom and me privately. My first thought was that there was something wrong with my baby. Instinctively, my hand went to cover my stomach. After everyone had left the room, the doctor pulled up a chair next to my mom and me. Mom reached over and took my hand. I could see by the look on her face that she had had the same thought.

"We have a couple of options here," the doctor told us. I was confused. Options?

"Anna is too far along to use a pill to stop the pregnancy." The doctor's words were not making sense to me. Why would I stop the pregnancy? That was exactly what I was trying not to do!

"I can refer her to a specialist who can take care of this." What?! I knew that my face must wear the horror I felt. I looked over at my mom and saw the same expression reflected. Then her face began to turn red, and she started to shake. She looked at me, as if to confirm that we were on the same page. I nodded. We stood together. I folded my hands over my growing belly, in a gesture of protection from what this "doctor" was suggesting.

You see, the year before, I had attended the required science class at the local public school. One of the things they taught us was basic reproduction. The material in the class did not go into great detail, but it did cover where babies came from. From it, we learned that it took genetic material from both the mother and the father to create a child. That meant that this baby had just as much of my blood as she had of her father's. This was my baby.

I could hear the growing rage in my mom's voice as she told the doctor that while we thanked him for his time, his "options" were not options at all, and we did not want, much less require, his referral. The doctor looked both shocked and confused as we left his office. That was fine with me. I was shocked and confused as well. What did he mean "take care of this"? How on earth would ending my pregnancy "take care of this"?

Our next stop was the police station. When we arrived, we were taken into separate rooms where we were told that our statements needed to be taken in order for them to prosecute my stepfather. Sitting alone in that room, my doubts and fears started creeping back in. What should I say? What did I need to do to protect my family?

I was alone for only a few moments before another police officer came in to talk with me. The first thing he told me was that I had nothing to be afraid of and he was there to help me. I wasn't sure I believed him, but everything was moving so quickly that I didn't know what else to do. I told him everything. He listened closely as I talked. Once in a while he would ask me a question, but for the most part, he just listened quietly to what I had to say. The longer I talked, the more his face changed. First angry, then sick, then both. Finally, after an hour and a half, it was done.

— 3 —

The next several weeks are still hard for me to describe. I remember certain events, but everything moved so fast that much of it is a blur. I remember my mom lost her job when she called in to tell them she needed to have a few days off to deal with the crisis we had found ourselves in. Consequently, we lost our home because we couldn't pay the rent. We moved into my Aunt Marsha's basement.

    We met with the lawyer who was to represent us at the trial, and again I had to confess all that had been done to me. Our lawyer was a kind man who reminded me of a large teddy bear. He warned us that I would have to testify against my stepfather, and that it would be hard, especially because I would have to repeat everything once more for the judge—and I would have to do it with my stepfather in the room. The fear I felt knowing that I would have to face him nearly paralyzed me. Not only would I have to tell of my abuse for a third time, but I would have to relive those moments with the object of my nightmares mere feet away.

I discovered that, like so many other things in life, the court system can be manipulated by emotions and appearances. I was told that it would help our case if I could wear a white dress to represent the innocence of my youth, bring a teddy bear, and cry while giving my testimony. I couldn't do all of it though. I went in the white dress with a bow in my hair. I held a teddy bear throughout the entire day. I answered every question the best I could.

But I couldn't cry. I refused to give him the satisfaction of seeing me broken once again. I needed for him to see that he had not broken me. I was strong enough to carry on, and I would get through this.

It seemed that the trial lasted forever, dragging on through the spring and well into the summer. It was finally determined that hard evidence was needed for a maximum conviction to be given. His confession and our testimonies were just not enough. Everyone settled down to wait until I gave birth so a paternity test could be administered. Time crept slowly on for all of us.

My mom tried to let me go back to school, but the other kids were cruel. They called me horrible names, and one even went so far as to break into my locker and etch the word "whore" into the door. My mom found me a tutor and arranged for me to be taught at home. Because of this, I received my first ever failing grade in science class. I didn't fail because my work was inadequate. I failed because I was unable to attend class and do the lab work.

We lost everything we had. Our home was already gone, and before long, our vehicle was taken as well. We had sold most of our belongings when we moved into my aunt's house, not only to save space, but also because we needed food and other essential items. The tiny amount of money my mom had from her job vanished quickly due to medical bills and the cost of caring for her children.

We desperately needed help.

I remember my mom going to the Baptist church my grandmother attended to ask for help. They called us liars and said we were not welcome there. She tried several other churches, with much the same result from each of them. Some called us liars; some said they would pray for us; and some said they just didn't have the resources. We sought church after church, but none could, or would, help us.

After all I had been through already, whatever faith I had left in God shattered when we were turned away by those churches. Those were supposed to be His people! *Why wouldn't they help us?* I determined that what I had learned as a child was a lie. God wouldn't help, nor would those who claimed to follow Him. We would do it on our own. I didn't need a God like that.

It wasn't until fairly recently that I understood the answer to my question. The reason no one would help was simple—they didn't want to see the truth. As long as they didn't have to see me and acknowledge what had happened, their world would be safe and comfortable. They could go on with their lives comfortably, with evil being some distant danger that they didn't have to face, much less fight. They knew what Jesus wanted them to do, but if they could convince themselves that I wasn't really the least of these and their neighbor, then their Savior's command to love me would not apply.

God, however, had not abandoned me. I just could not see it at the time. Of all the "friends" I had before the truth came to light, there were two who stuck by me through it all. Their names were Alisa and Courtney, and they were enough. We spent nearly every weekend together. Movies were our favorite escape, and we could usually be found either at the theater or at one another's homes in front of the television. We would stay up all night, developing dreams, watching movies, and eating whatever we could get our hands on. In this way, I had a piece of childhood to cling to and call my own, even though most of childhood had long ago been lost to me.

Even now, 18 years later, when I look back on my pregnancy, those are the memories I cherish the most. Those dear girls didn't look at me like I was a monster. They didn't avert their eyes when I walked by. They held my hand and walked through my valley with me. They defended me against those who sought to tear me down. They made me laugh when all I wanted to do was cry. I tremble at the thought of where I would have been had God not put them into my life. Darkness cannot stand the light, and with Alisa and Courtney, darkness had no place to hide.

— 4 —

I grew a great deal that summer. I didn't get any taller, but I filled out quickly. In early spring, I weighed around 75 pounds. By the time my daughter was born, I had gained nearly 80 more. I developed stretch marks all over my body. We did the best we could to ease the pains of the growing baby, using vitamin E and lavender oils to make my skin more elastic. Still, there was only so much we could do to alleviate the changes.

Because I was so young—only 13—I was deemed a high-risk pregnancy. I needed to go to the hospital for regular checkups and ultrasounds to make sure that both my baby and I were doing well. Early on, my mom and I had discussed the possibility of giving my child up for adoption because of my youth. Given the situation we were in, I thought it might be best if she were raised by someone who would be able to provide more for her than I could. However, during one of those first ultrasounds, I got to see her. I saw her little face and hands. I heard her heartbeat and watched her sucking her thumb. I fell in love with her. This little being inside me became my whole world.

Due to the risks to my daughter and myself, I was not allowed much activity. My mom and aunt took me to the public swimming pool once, but the reaction of the public there ensured that we would not do it again. I did a lot of reading, even finding my daughter's name in the pages of a book, one of those cheesy teenage romances that I hated to admit I loved. The name of the book was *A New Face in the Mirror* by Nola Carson. I named her "Josey Ann" after the main character—a tough tomboy who loved to work on cars. She was strong and independent and not afraid to stand up for herself and her family. She had a big heart and a wonderful sense of humor. She was the girl I wished I could have been, and who I prayed my daughter could grow to be.

I had to have new clothes, and we had to prepare for the blessed arrival of my baby. As such, my mom and I went to yard sales, using money given to us by friends and family. It took some time and a great deal of bargaining, but we finally acquired the necessities. We found clothing for both of us, a stroller, a crib, and a few blankets. It wasn't much, but it was enough. All I needed was enough to get us through.

I went into labor in the early hours of Friday, July 28, 1995. However, it took me several hours to realize what was happening. My mom and I had been sharing a room in my aunt's basement. My back was aching horribly, so I got out of bed to walk around, hoping to relieve some of the tension without waking my mom. It was about three in the morning and dark. The room was cloaked with silence. As I paced the room, I massaged my back and berated myself for being such a wimp. It was just a little back ache. Women had been dealing with this kind of problem during pregnancy for centuries, right?

The pain grew and began to stretch its fingers towards my stomach. After a while I began to have trouble walking. It briefly crossed my mind that I might be in labor, but I dismissed the thought quickly. It was only the end of July, and my baby wasn't due until the middle of September. It was way too early for this to be labor! So I continued to pace, and the pain intensified. Eventually, I couldn't bear to stand any longer, so I sat on the edge of the bed and wrapped my arms around my large belly and the little girl inside.

I must have made some kind of noise in my distress because my mom awoke. She stood and turned on the light, asking what was wrong. A sharp pain hit me, and I had trouble answering. She knelt by my side and placed her hand on my stomach. She could feel it tightening, and I bit my lip to keep from crying out. After the anguish subsided a bit, she asked me how long this had been going on. When I told her, she rushed upstairs to wake my aunt. They packed me up quickly and sped me to the hospital where the doctor confirmed that I was indeed in labor.

After thoroughly examining the progression of my labor and the general health of my daughter and myself, the doctors decided that they were not equipped to care for a child giving birth to a child. They said that my mom could come with me, but I would have to be transferred to a hospital that could better deal with a pregnancy such as mine. An ambulance was called, and I was transported to the airport and then flown to Primary Children's Hospital in Salt Lake City. While I was scared about the birth and what my body was going through, I had to admit that I was excited about this part. I had always wanted to fly but had never had the opportunity before then. Unfortunately, I was unable to experience any of it, as the medications they had given me knocked me out until well after we landed.

When I awoke, I was in another ambulance, now in Salt Lake City. I don't remember being checked in or even moving into my room. I remember they didn't want me to get out of bed for any reason whatsoever. Because my daughter was coming so early, they wanted to do everything possible to keep her inside longer and increase her chances for survival. I was given several shots, some for me and others for her. I was given pain medications, and something to drastically slow the labor. Through me, she was given steroids to develop her lungs.

I remember a doctor coming in once with several other people. He explained to me that they would like to observe my treatment because they were in training. It occurred to me then that I couldn't be the only girl that this happened to. It was such a simple thing, the doctor asking for those students to be able to observe. But it meant that they were planning on helping others that were like me. Suddenly, I didn't feel so alone.

I laid in that hospital bed all weekend, trying my best to wait patiently. My mom brought me books and magazines to read, and I was able to watch television. But I really just wanted to get up. I was bored. I was 13 and about to give birth to a very premature baby, but the feeling I remember the most at that time was sheer boredom. Don't believe me? Try getting any other 13-year-old to stay in one spot for three days. Don't even let her up to go to the bathroom. It won't be long until she is begging you for the privilege of going outside or—believe it—doing chores around the house. She will be willing to do almost anything just to get up and move around.

It was this boredom that started everything. On Monday morning, my mom left me alone for a while. She needed to get herself something to eat and clean up. She had been with me in my hospital room the whole time. Lying there in bed, I thought I would lose my mind if something didn't happen soon. I looked around the room for something to occupy my time. I didn't want to read anymore, nor did I want to watch television. What else could I do?

Then I saw it. The call button for the nurses' station. I knew I shouldn't. Really I did. But I reached over and pushed it anyways. Only a moment later, a nurse came rushing in. I had to come up with a reason for why I had called her and fast! So I said the first thing that came to my mind.

"I think it's time."

So, she did what any good nurse would do—she checked. Then she looked up at me from the bottom of my bed and told me I was right. While I was lying there in shock, she ran out to call the doctor and send for my mom. I was panicked. I was just kidding! I didn't mean it! Apparently, my pain medication had worked a little too well. I had not noticed, but I was contracting regularly and was fully dilated when I called her. Oh, what a blessing is the providence of God!

By the time my mom reached me, they had already taken me into the delivery room. I was terrified. I begged my mom to stop this. I told her I didn't want to do this. She grabbed my hand, squeezed it, and told me it was too late. I had to finish.

I remember very little of the next several hours. I remember that the lights in that room were blinding. It hurt so much, but I had to keep pushing. I remember the doctor telling me at one point that I had to stop pushing because there was something wrong. I heard the word "forceps," and I saw my mom turn white.

I AM THE EXCEPTION

The pain was excruciating. All the heartache, torment, and fear I had felt in the past materialized, in physical form, ripping through my body like a tempest through a ship. I was certain my little skiff was sinking! I felt more of that incredible pain and then some relief.

I could hear the doctors and the nurses talking while one of them ran across the room with something in her arms. Surely that wasn't my baby?! Wasn't she supposed to be crying? The person on the other side of the room was moving frantically, and after just a few moments, they quickly pushed a cart out of the room. I remember them telling me I had a little girl, but they took her so fast! I didn't even get to hold her.

I remember hearing someone who I thought was the doctor speaking with my mom. What he said wasn't clear to me. I only caught disjointed words here and there.

"Not breathing... NICU... be alright."

I tried to pay attention, as I was sure it was important for me to hear what he was saying. But I was just so tired, and I was fading quickly. The pain, fear, and apprehension all slipped away as I succumbed to the darkness.

When I finally woke up, it was several hours later. I was back in my room. My mom was sitting next to me, and it looked like she had been praying and crying the entire time I was sleeping. I was still groggy, so it took a few moments for the events of that morning to return to me. I looked around the room, but there was no sign of my baby. What did they do with my baby?

"Mom, where is she?" I croaked. She told me that my daughter was not breathing when she was born. Fear rushed into my body.

"It's alright," she told me. "They have her in with the other babies that have problems. They are taking good care of her. She's going to be okay."

I still wasn't sure. I needed to see her, to hold her. It had been nearly eight hours since my baby girl had been born, and I had not seen her yet. I tried to get up, but I was so sore, and I was still attached to all the machines that monitored my health. Only a mother could understand my desperation at that moment—I was frantic, yet I was stuck.

I had my mom call for a nurse to come and help because I was determined to see my little girl as soon as I possibly could. While we waited for the nurse to arrive, my mom brushed out my hair. She soothed me, telling me again and again how well I did and how proud of me she was.

Finally, at long last, the nurse arrived with a wheelchair. She unhooked me from most of the equipment and helped me move to the chair. She asked me if I was ready to go. For such a simple question, I had a difficult time giving her an honest answer. I wanted to see Josey more than anything, but I was also terrified of the condition I would find her in.

She had been born so early. What if she was too small to survive? What if I had done something to hurt her? What if I did something now that would hurt her? And, like a thief in the night come to steal my joy, came the thought I could not keep out—what if she looks like him? I knew she was an innocent baby and that she was her own person. But deep down, I wondered.

I tried to pay attention to where we were going when the nurse wheeled me out. The medications used to numb my pain were still in my system, and the next moments moved slowly, like the disjointed frames of a drawn-out dream. All I could see were white walls and corridors that seemed to stretch eternally in front of me. The antiseptic smell of the hospital burned in my nose. I could hear the sound of the wheelchair rolling across the tile and the nurse's shoes squeaking with each step she took. Although I could not see her, I knew that my mom was right behind me as well.

Finally, we arrived at the Neonatal Intensive Care Unit (NICU). Before I was allowed to enter the room where my daughter was, the nurses showed me how to properly wash my hands to minimize exposure to germs that her little body was not yet equipped to fight. They warned me that she would have several tubes and wires attached to her to help her breathe and monitor her vitals. I was exceedingly apprehensive by the time they allowed me into the nursery. With all the rules they had given me before I could see her, I worried that I might hurt her.

The nurse wheeled me through the door, and the first things I saw were the machines. As she pushed me further into the room, I saw the babies that the machines were attached to. It was so quiet. I could hear the beeps and humming of the equipment. I was deeply unsettled by the silence from these precious babies. I think the silence worried me the most. In all the movies I had ever seen, the hospital nurseries were noisy. You could always hear the infants crying, sniffling, and making sweet baby noises. I heard none of that there.

I was taken across the room to a small plastic box that held my daughter. The first thing I noticed was how tiny she was. I could see her little chest rise and fall with each breath she took. She encompassed every hope, every dream that I had held for all those months tied into one precious little package. I loved her instantly. One of the nurses told me that my baby had been using a breathing tube earlier that day, but she had spit it out not long before I arrived. My little girl was breathing on her own! That bit of news was the best I had heard in a very long time.

If she could breathe on her own, then maybe she really would be alright.

One of the nurses that would be taking care of my baby came over and introduced herself. She told us that they were so excited to have my child there. She was big enough that they could play with her! I remember looking at her again, seeing how small she was. Then I looked around the room at some of the other infants. She was indeed one of the largest there. The thought amazed me. How could these tiny little creatures survive?

I tried to pay attention to what the nurse was saying about what they were doing with my daughter, but my attention kept moving back to my little girl. I was sure my mom would tell me everything later. Right then, I just wanted to see her, study her, and reassure myself that she was fine. I counted each of her little tiny fingers and toes. I studied the little bit of hair that she had on her tiny head. It was so fine and so fair that you could barely see that she had any.

Her facial features were also tiny, but proportionate to the rest of her little body. Her eyes were a dark blue, but I had been informed that her eyes might change color as time passed. Her skin seemed slightly yellowed, and the nurse informed me that she had a mild case of jaundice, but the blue lights around her box would help. She also had two slight dents on each side of her head that worried me. Again, the nurse reassured me that the dents would heal. She said that the birth had been difficult, and the doctor had used delivery forceps.

Finally, the moment I had been waiting for—the nurse asked me if I would like to hold her. Yes! More than anything! I felt as though that one little action was going to change the course of my entire life. I knew that with my baby in my arms, nothing would ever be the same. It seemed that time crawled to a stop as the nurse wrapped her in a blanket, making sure that she was secure.

As the nurse laid her in my arms and I felt her slight frame against mine for the first time, I realized I was right. Nothing would ever be the same. There was nothing I wouldn't do for this precious child. I looked up, surprised that the rest of the planet had not changed at the same time I did. I counted and re-counted her fingers and toes.

After all the grief and fear that had shipwrecked my body, after all the hope and desire that had swept through and left me broken, here was an emotion that I had never felt in this measure. Deeper, wider, and stronger than all the others, it took root in my being and settled into all my corners and all my closets. From my fingers, full of life, to my ribs, expanding with adoration, all the way to my feet and into my soul, I felt it. I loved her.

Her little hand wrapped around my finger and my heart at the same time. I had not known that it was possible to feel any emotion so strongly. Although I couldn't understand why, I felt tears filling my eyes. Now I could understand those stories about mothers dying to protect their children. I knew in that moment that I would do the same, without question. The frightening part was that I knew that dying would have been easier. Instead, I would have to live and fight for her.

— 5 —

The nurse told me that I could breastfeed my baby if I wished, but I would need to use a pump, as she was still too small to suckle. She would have to have the milk given to her through a feeding tube. My mom told the nurse that would not be something I could do, as I would be starting back to school in a few weeks. The nurse said that that was perfectly understandable, so she gave me instructions on what I would need to do in order to dry up my breast milk.

All too soon, I had to go back to my room. I was unbelievably tired, and my mom told me that I really needed to eat something. I had not yet done so that day. Before I had to leave my baby, I kissed the top of her little head, and vowed that I would do everything I could to be the best mommy for her that I could possibly be. As the nurse took my little girl from my arms, I knew that my heart went back into that box with her. As we were leaving the room, one of the nurses stopped me.

"Have you chosen a name for her?"

"Yes," I replied, "her name is Josey Ann."

I was only allowed to stay at the hospital for a couple more days, and then I had to return home. As I no longer required medical attention, the hospital could not allow me to stay with my daughter. I was terrified to leave her. My home was nearly a five hour drive away. We did not have the money to drive back and forth each day, nor did we have the money for me to stay in Salt Lake City. Even before we left, I was making calls, trying to find ways to get back to Salt Lake from the day I had to leave until the day she got to come home.

My grandmother was a manager at a hotel in Vernal, and we discovered that she had a conference she had to attend during one of those weekends. That was the only time I would be able to return to see my baby girl.

My heart was breaking the morning I had to leave. I spent the first part of the morning in my room crying. I didn't think I could do it. How was I supposed to leave my heart at that hospital while I returned home? I was desperately trying to figure out a way to stay, but could think of nothing. Finally, the nurse came and told me that I could go to the nursery to spend a few more precious hours with my daughter.

In what seemed like no time at all, my mom was telling me that it was time to go. We had to head home. We gathered the few possessions we had, and loaded them into my aunt's car. She had driven there to pick us up earlier that morning. Throughout the drive home, my mom kept telling me that it wouldn't be long before Josey would be able to come back with us. Besides, we had a great deal to get done before we were ready to bring her back.

I knew she was right. My aunt had told my mom about a trailer home that she thought we might be able to move into, but it would require a huge amount of time and work, especially if we were to have it ready to bring a newborn home. I also had to enroll into junior high school. I was not looking forward to that part at all. After the way I had been treated the previous year, I was fearful of returning to school. I did not want to face the other kids, or even the teachers.

I knew that I had done nothing wrong. That did not change the fact that I would be ridiculed and shunned by those who saw me. I knew this. I also knew that I had to do it anyway, not because the state laws required it, but because I now had to begin working toward a future in which I could care for that cherished child I had left at the hospital only hours before.

I did not want to depend on the state for the rest of my life. I wanted to be someone my daughter could look up to and be proud of. I wanted to be able to support her without having to depend on anyone else. I wasn't sure what I was going to do, but I knew that I would need an excellent education to do it. So with a tremulous but determined heart, I decided that I would face whatever came my way, and I would do it for my daughter.

My aunt had found us a home. We spent the next several days moving into a three-bedroom trailer on the outskirts of town. My mom and I decided that, at least for a while, I would share a room with her. That way she could help me care for Josey. I had no idea what a baby would need from me or how to even begin caring for one. My siblings and I were close enough in age that I had never even been around small children.

We didn't have much to prepare, but we did the best we could. We had acquired a crib and placed it next to my bed. We washed and sanitized all of Josey's bottles. Her clothing was laundered and put into a small dresser. We had a rocking chair that went into the bedroom as well, for those midnight feedings. While it wasn't much, it overwhelmed me at the time.

The entire time we were working, I missed my little girl. I knew that she was growing more and more each day, and it was breaking my heart that I couldn't watch it. I wanted to be there every second to watch each move she made, and to know exactly what was happening with her. I'm sure the nurses at the hospital must have been gifted with extra doses of patience. I called them at least once a day, sometimes more, just to see if there were any changes. Each time they would answer my questions and reassure me that Josey was healthy and growing well.

About two weeks after I had left Josey at the hospital, I had the opportunity to go back and see her. I drove to Salt Lake City with my grandmother, hoping to spend just a few hours with Josey. Grandma took me to the hospital before her meetings. I spent a few hours with my daughter, watching her, talking to her, and just holding her before Grandma picked me up. We went out to eat, and then she took me back to the hospital for a short visit before we had to return to the hotel. All too soon the weekend was over, and I had to leave Josey once again.

By the time I returned home, I only had a couple of weeks left before school was supposed to start. It was time to enroll. While I said nothing to my mom about my fears, I think she could sense my trepidation. Before we left the house, she gave my hand a squeeze and told me again that everything would be fine. If she could have, I think my mom would have protected me from everything and everyone. As a mother, I now understand this. Unfortunately, it is impossible to perfectly protect our children. Somehow, the world always seeps in.

— 6 —

When we arrived in the office of the junior high school, my mom had to fill out the usual paperwork required for every student. The problem didn't come until my mom had to explain to them why I did not attend the final portion of my previous year of school. While my mom explained the situation to the vice principal, I waited for the bomb to drop. And it did.

Once my mom had finished speaking, the vice principle decided that it was his turn. He told my mom that there was an alternative school down the street, and that she should consider enrolling me there. That way, I could be with my "own kind." He didn't think that I would fit in with the "respectable" kids at the regular school. After hearing what he said, I thought he might be right. After all, if he was an example of "respectable," why would I want to surround myself with people like him?

Mom didn't agree. She asked me to step out into the hallway for a few minutes while she had a talk with him. I did as she asked and found myself a nice patch of tile outside of the office door. Inside, I could hear her raising her voice with each word she spoke. The door was closed, so I could not understand what she was saying, but I could imagine it fairly well. For a brief moment, I almost felt bad for the poor man.

As I sat there, I tried to picture my little girl's face. I needed to hold on to my reasons for wanting to attend this school. I knew that I would receive a better education here than at the alternative school. However, that man's words and attitude made me doubt for a moment whether it would be worth it. As Josey's precious little face formed in my mind, I knew she was worth it. It did not matter what anyone else said. She was my invaluable treasure, and for her I would put up with their ignorance.

After our encounter at the junior high school, my mom decided we needed to go visit my aunt for a while. She didn't speak much while we were driving, but that was good with me. I didn't know what to say either. If the adults were that bad, what would the kids be like? How was I going to make it through the coming year, much less the years that followed?

While my mom vented with my aunt over a cup of coffee, I sat on her porch and just observed the world around me. I felt so alone. I didn't fit in anywhere. While my family tried to be supportive, they couldn't understand what I was going through. Alisa and Courtney were amazing, but they didn't get it either, and no one else even tried.

My heart cried out to God again. I kept hearing that He was a loving and forgiving God, so why couldn't I see it? Where was He? I didn't know what I could have done to deserve the wrath that I felt had been poured upon me. As I sat on the porch with tears trailing down my cheeks, I shook my fists at Him once again. If He existed, I wanted nothing to do with Him.

Morale improved for the entire family the next day. The hospital called and told us that Josey was nearly ready to be released. If everything continued to go well, she would be able to come home the day before I started the seventh grade. I was simultaneously ecstatic and deeply terrified. There was so much to do!

My mom had taken me to the county health office so I could enroll with WIC—a government program that assists mothers in providing for their children—to help with the expense of baby formula until we could find a way to obtain some income. With Josey coming home in a matter of days, I had to go to the store and make sure that she would have something to eat.

My little sister accompanied me into the store. It took me some time to figure out what I needed to get, but I did eventually find everything. As we made our way to the checkout line, we talked about the coming school year, and how excited we were that my baby girl was coming home. Everything was going fine until I handed the cashier the WIC check to pay for the formula.

The woman told me that the mother had to be the one who used the check. When I informed her that I was the mother, the lecture began. She told me how girls my age should not be "messing around" with boys, and I should be ashamed of myself. As she continued to talk, I could feel my face flush red with embarrassment. I thought about trying to explain myself to her, but decided it would not help the situation. My sister just stood next to me, looking shocked. Until that point, she had not observed how others had begun to see me. Finally, the cashier rang everything through, and we left.

On our way back to the car, I commanded my sister not to say anything to my mom about what had happened. Of course, she didn't listen. At this news, my mother came unhinged. Again.

She instructed us to wait in the car, and she stormed into the store. As we waited, the cashier's words reverberated in my head. They tore another little piece out of my soul. Maybe I really was a bad person. Maybe I did deserve this. After all, I hadn't met any other girls in a situation like mine, so maybe I had done something to warrant my circumstances. I sat in the car and wept.

It was nearly a half hour later when my mom finally returned to us. She didn't say much, but she still looked furious. She was muttering something under her breath, but I was unable to make out her words. When my sister asked what had happened, all mom would tell us is that the cashier would be much nicer if we ever saw her again. I didn't really care if she would be nicer the next time. She had already told me her opinion, and I had no desire to encounter her again.

The reality of how I would be treated from then on was starting to dawn on me. It was becoming more and more obvious that people were unable to look past surface appearances to see the reality of what was going on. For a 13-year-old girl, this was a hard concept to accept, but life wasn't giving me many options. I had known for some time that the world could be hard, but I was just now learning how cruel the people in it could be.

I couldn't understand why people would react that way just because I had a baby. I had not hurt anyone. Even if I had done the things that they implied, how did that excuse their attitudes? There was no love in their rebuke. They offered no hope or forgiveness, only condemnation. There was a darkness in my heart that had begun with what my stepfather had done to me. Each time that I encountered another person like that cashier, that darkness grew, covering me as shadows cover the land when the evening sneaks in. There were times I thought the darkness would just swallow me whole, and I would disappear forever. Sometimes, I really wished it would.

— 7 —

As the day of Josey's arrival drew closer, both my excitement and my nerves were magnified with every passing hour. When I saw her and held her at the hospital, there were nurses and medical professionals to help if I did something wrong. What would happen when she was home with me? I was terrified that I would hurt her and that I wouldn't be the mother I knew she deserved.

I often wondered if I had made the right choice in not giving her up for adoption. I knew there were families out there who would love her and who could offer her materially more than I could, but I was selfish. I wanted my daughter with me. I needed to see her. To those who have never been there, it may be hard to understand, but after all I had experienced, I needed something good, and she was that good.

We had done all we could at the house to prepare for her arrival. Arrangements had been made for my mom and me to borrow a vehicle to travel to Salt Lake City and back. The infant car seat had been tested and installed. All I had to do was wait. Unfortunately, patience was not my strongest virtue, so those last few days were torture.

Finally, the day arrived. I was up long before the sun, anxious to be on our way. I couldn't wait to see my little girl again. Despite my impatience, we still had to wait until my aunt arrived to care for my brother and sister while we were traveling. By nine o'clock, we were on the road.

Once we arrived at the hospital, I discovered that there was a great deal I had to know before Josey could be released. The nurses had to teach me about various aspects of how to care for a premature baby, and I had to demonstrate different techniques to show them that I understood. I had to know what medications she required, when to give them to her, and their proper dosage. I had to demonstrate how to hold and feed her properly. They also informed us that because of our situation, there would be people from the state who would check in on us at home from time to time to be sure that we were all doing well. The staff also had to perform a safety check on the infant seat to make sure that it was up to code and installed properly.

I was beginning to believe that we would have to spend the night in the city, when they finally released her to us. At last, my little girl was coming home! Although Mom and I were both physically, mentally, and emotionally exhausted, we began the long drive back to Vernal. We had to hurry, as school was going to start for me the next morning. I was in high spirits. I had my baby girl. After everything that had happened, I finally knew in my spirit that all would be well.

I don't think I slept at all that night. Between watching Josey sleep and fearing what would happen when I walked through the doors of the junior high, my mind refused to settle down. This was the first year I had ever dreaded going to school. It had always been an escape for me, a safe haven away from the horror at home. Now everything was backwards, and I was unsure of how to handle it. The thought of facing my classmates in just a few short hours was making me physically ill. I could feel my stomach churning as I lay in my bed.

Yet, as I watched my daughter's gentle breathing as she slept, I knew what I had to do. I just didn't want to do it. To this day, I cannot recall a time when I felt as cowardly as I did that night. I realized even then that my thoughts were those of a victim, and that made me angry and resentful. My stepfather may have been in prison, but my life was still being influenced by him.

My mom had a saying that she would frequently use whenever dealing with a stressful situation: "Just put on your big girl panties and deal with it."

Such simple words, but I learned to live by them. Life is rarely, if ever, fair or just. I had learned already that life was brutal, painful, and cruel at times. There are countless times when a person finds himself in a difficult situation. Sometimes he put himself there; other times it is through no fault of his own. That does not change the fact that the situation exists and needs to be dealt with rightly.

I was quickly learning that while I could not always control the situations I found myself in, I could control what I did about them. I decided to take a "fake it 'til you make it" approach to the way people were treating me. Just because they were treating me like trash didn't mean I had to show that their words affected me. I simply needed to find a way to silence that little part of me that wanted to be normal and liked. I did not know how I was going to do that. But by that time, I had become very good at hiding what was going on in my head. I had years of practice.

I got up the next morning exhausted but determined to face, with head held high, whatever the day had in store. After I was dressed and had Josey fed and changed, my mom told us that she wanted to get pictures taken of each of us before we left for school. My aunt had let us borrow a camera so we could get a few photos of Josey's first days at home, and mom was anxious to start capturing the moments. So my brother, sister and I took turns posing. I got a couple extra shots so we could have some of me with my baby girl.

Staring into her precious little face, I reminded myself of all the reasons I needed to go to school. I gave her little body one last squeeze and handed her to my mom. It was time to go. At least I knew I had two friends who would stand by me through this. That would be enough. As always, what I was given would sustain me.

The next several days were rough, but I did as I had determined and stood with my back straight and my chin high. The name-calling and "practical jokes" were not the most enjoyable aspects of school. But I will admit that I almost preferred those who were openly hostile to those who would stare at me and then whisper amongst themselves. The openly adverse kids could be dismissed as mere bullies. The others made me feel ashamed, though I was never quite sure why.

Slowly, I started to settle into a routine. My life was far from glamorous and looked nothing like those that I read about or saw in the movies, but I was content. I went to school in the mornings and then spent time with my princess in the afternoons. Occasionally, I would spend a weekend night with Courtney and Alisa at the movies.

We made a few happy memories. There was a cemetery about a block away from our home, and I would put Josey in her stroller and walk there. It became my favorite place to escape. While some people found the cemetery creepy, I found it peaceful. There was no one there to judge or criticize. I didn't have to be artificial for anyone. When I was upset, I could cry, and when happy, I could laugh—and no one said anything to me.

Taking care of a baby was hard, and I had no idea what I was doing. I don't know what I would have done without my mom. Most of the time I was terrified of hurting my little girl. The nurses at the hospital had taught me how to hold, feed, and change her, but I had no idea what to do with her. I didn't know how to play with a baby. I didn't know what to do if she was crying after she had been fed and changed. I was still just a child. I was lost.

A few weeks after we brought her home, she began crying all the time. Nothing we did would soothe her. My mom and I were both exhausted from being up all night. We made an appointment with her doctor, and we found out that she had colic. I had no idea what that meant, but my mom seemed to. We went to the store and bought a bottle of something she said would help. It did help, to a point, but Josey was still fussy a great deal of the time.

To make matters worse, I had started having nightmares and flashbacks. Maybe it was because of the exhaustion of caring for a child while being a full-time student, or maybe it was because I was so used to living in fear that my mind couldn't accept the fact that I was now safe. The smallest things could trigger the memories. A smell, a song on the radio, a flash of light, even a stranger could send my mind hurling into the darkness again.

The court had ordered me to see a counselor once a week, but it didn't help much. She told me that I was dealing with things very well, but she couldn't see inside my head or my heart. She couldn't see that I was falling slowly into madness. I wanted to fight for my little girl, but there were times when it was just more than I could take.

I remember returning home from school one day after some of the other kids had been particularly merciless. Mom was in the shower, and I was in the kitchen preparing a bottle for Josey. I cannot remember what triggered the flashback that time, but when I emerged from it, I had a knife in my hands. I was sitting under the table, and had tried cutting my wrists. I became aware that my mom had her hands on my shoulders and was shaking me.

I tried to tell her what was going on, but I couldn't. I couldn't formulate words for what was in my head, but I think she knew. After taking the knife from me, she ran into the bedroom and brought Josey from her crib. I remember mom laying my baby girl in my lap, and telling me that I could not possibly be so selfish as to take my own life. She told me I was stronger than that, and by continuing down that road, I was only letting him win.

She was right. As I sat there looking at my little girl, I knew mom was right. The more I allowed everyone and everything to get to me, the more victorious he was. Looking at my Josey, I tickled her little feet. She giggled, and I wondered what I needed to do to rid myself of this darkness within me. I thought I knew what needed to be done. I just had no idea how to go about doing it.

So I did the only thing I knew to do, and I pushed the memories further down into my head. I stood on them and stomped them into a little box and then shoved them into a dark corner of my mind. When there were times that the memories tried to resurface, I would take it out in my writings or perhaps in my drawings, but I could not let the memories control me anymore.

— 8 —

As the school year progressed, I learned how to deal with the other kids better. Some, I would just ignore. For others, I would have to take a different approach— I would use their snide comments and rude remarks to motivate myself. I would prove them wrong about the things they said. I would work harder, get better grades, and make something of myself. Then they wouldn't laugh at me anymore.

While life at school did improve over time, things at home were still going downhill. Mom was unable to find work, as she had to take care of the baby during the mornings, and take care of my siblings and me after school. The emotional stress and strain that she was under, I believe, would have broken most women. Even now, I don't know how she pulled herself through those dark days. There were times when we went without heat or hot water because we couldn't afford to pay the bills.

We managed until after school ended that year, and then we lost our home again. My aunt had moved, so we had no family to turn to. We spent a couple of weeks in a friend's garage, and then my mom couldn't take it anymore. She called my father and asked him for help. After negotiating the terms of his assistance, he agreed.

According to the negotiations, my father would not be allowed to drink any more. My parents would be remarried, and we would move into his house. We would have a permanent home at last. Not having to worry about where we were going to live would be a huge relief to my mom and me. While I, like my mom, was initially wary of the arrangement, I decided that the benefits far outweighed the costs. And maybe my father could change. Maybe I could finally have that family I had dreamed of for so long. Still, I was afraid to hope for it.

We moved back to the small town of Manila, next to the Flaming Gorge. Josey was nearly a year old, and I was fourteen. My brother and sister were so excited. By my parents reuniting, a large part of our family that had been lost with the divorce was now returned to us. We had aunts, uncles, cousins, and grandparents whom we barely remembered, and now they were frequent visitors. We rediscovered our brothers and sisters whom we had not seen in years.

I will admit that I was scared of my father for the first several months we were there. After what I had experienced with my stepfather, I expected more abuse to begin at any time. It still had not fully registered in my mind that not all men were like that. I kept waiting for the worst to happen. It never did though, and I started to relax.

Not long after the wedding, my father started taking my family into the woods to help him work, and I discovered escape like I had never known before. I found I could lose myself not only in my work, but in the woods as well. I found a peace in those mountains that I had only previously caught glimpses of. For the first time in many years, I found what it was like to be happy. I savored the sweet seclusion from the torment of the outside world.

Each morning, I would get up and help my father collect firewood, house logs, and fence posts from among the trees on his timber sale. We would cut them down, drag them to the log deck with his old skidding tractor, and cut them to length. Then we would load them. I loved my work. It felt honest and real. We were providing people with a product that they needed, and I was able to live in the woods while doing it.

After a solid day's work, we played. Sometimes we would go swimming at the lake; sometimes we would go fishing; and other times I would take off into the woods by myself. I ran, climbed trees, hiked, and explored. I listened to the birds and learned the local vegetation. I discovered which plants were edible, and learned the habits of the local wildlife. While I still held a great deal of animosity towards God (how could I forgive Him?), I fell in love with His creation.

I developed a reputation among my father's customers for having a strong work ethic. I was offered a job as a waitress at a summer retreat in the Uinta Mountains the following spring. The only disadvantage to this job was that I would have to live at the camp during the summer. This meant I would be away from my daughter and the rest of my family, whom I was growing to love.

After a great deal of deliberation, I decided to take the job anyway. Even though I would be away from Josey, I felt I needed to be doing something to start earning some money to help with family expenses. This would put me one step closer to being able to provide for my daughter. Looking back, I know my mom and father never meant for me to feel like I needed to provide for myself. They wanted to take care of me and Josey, but it was something that I felt I needed to do. I was still trying to prove my own worth, even if it was just to myself.

Besides, with a new school year at a new school steadily approaching, I needed something to look forward to. I did not want to go back to school. I had made it through the previous year and did not want to repeat that experience at any level. I was a coward. I liked my life of living in the woods away from everyone. For the most part, my family accepted me, and I didn't have to worry about anyone while I was enjoying the outdoors. If I could have avoided other people for the rest of my life, I would have.

I tried using the same motivational techniques that I had used when preparing for school the previous year, but they just were not working. At least when I had done it the last time, I had two friends I knew would stand by me throughout the days. Now I knew no one. I would have to face this completely alone. But, like many things in life, I did not get to choose whether to go back to school. It was decided for me. I just had to deal with it.

As fall rolled in, we spent more time at home. Because we lived outside town, I could still at least partially escape from society. I discovered a small cave on the other side of the hill behind our house where my grandfather had played when he was younger. This became my new retreat. I would go there often to draw or write or even just to think. In this sanctuary, I could be away from everyone.

We had very little contact with the town's residents. Of the few I had met, I was surprised at how many remembered me from when I was a little girl. I suppose small towns are like that. Especially Manila. It seemed like the majority of the people I came in contact with were relatives in one way or another.

Many of them already knew of our situation, but they didn't make a big deal of it, and this surprised me. We had only a few people say nasty things, but they did it more discreetly. We had a few notes left in our mailbox, and we were stared at when no one knew we were looking, but we were not confronted like we had been before. Most of the residents had known my parents since they were children, and we were accepted back into the community because we were family.

Even with the partially positive reactions of the adults I had met, I was unsure about the kids at school. Often children will act differently when they are away from their parents, and I was afraid of repeating the last years' experience.

Once again, the night before the first day of school, I was wide awake. Once again I was imagining all the awful things that the other kids were going to say and do once I walked through those doors. I briefly thought about asking God to help me, but I decided that if He wouldn't help me when I was most desperate, then there was little chance He would help me with something so small. At the very least, I packed an extra book and a drawing pad into my backpack just in case I needed to hide for a while. I reminded myself of all the reasons I needed to finish my education. I also reminded myself that I needed to go, if only to have access to the town's only library, which was located in the high school.

My new school was smaller than any I had previously attended. There were fewer than 100 kids in the sixth through 12th grades, and we were all in the same building. The school consisted of four hallways, seven classrooms, a cafeteria, gym, boys' and girls' shower rooms, and a library. Only two of the hallways held lockers. At least I wouldn't have to worry about getting lost.

I wasn't very friendly to the other kids that first day. I expected the worst from everyone and didn't want to give them the chance to prove that they might not be as bad as I had imagined. Several kids tried to talk to me, but I took most of what they said the wrong way. I couldn't see it at the time, but I was embittered from what had happened before. I saw everyone through the filter of my hardened heart.

It took me several weeks before I could see that these kids weren't as bad as the ones from the city. They were good country folk, who honestly didn't judge me for things that were beyond my control. Granted, a small handful were unpleasant, but for the most part it was a nice change. I think that it helped that most of them were either family or friends of the family.

I made a few friends, although I didn't allow anyone to get as close as Courtney and Alisa had been. I worked hard on my grades and joined several groups. I was on the Academic Decathlon team, as well as the dance team. I was in a couple of the school plays and attended most of the dances. While I was never good at playing sports, I enjoyed attending the basketball games. For the most part, I was able to function as a normal teenager.

One day during my junior year, I truly came to appreciate the community that a small town like ours offered. A lady from the city came to our school to talk with the seniors about pregnancy, adoption, and abortion. She informed many of the students that having a child at that point in their lives could ruin their futures. They had such great lives ahead of them, she said, and should they face a pregnancy they would be well advised to either abort or give the child up for adoption. Abortion, in her mind, was the best option, as it would make it easier for the mother to continue in school if she didn't have to endure nine months of pregnancy. Of course, before the lecturer left for the day, I was notified by my classmates about her presence, and my mom and I were allowed to sit in on one of her "classes." Afterward, Mom and I had a talk with this woman about what she had said to the class.

We told her about how these kids knew us and what we had been through. They saw that even in the worst circumstances, the resulting baby was an amazing gift. The kids at this school did not need nor want her opinions on how a baby could ruin the life of a young girl. They had witnessed first-hand how that child could help that girl to overcome her situation, rather than being destroyed by it.

Several of the other kids stood with us at that moment, and I remember how thankful I was that they were there and willing to stand by me. I remember one of the seniors giving me a hug and telling me how proud of me she was. And I remember thinking that maybe we really had done it. Maybe we had beaten our circumstances, and my stepfather didn't control us anymore. That was the first time I ever publicly spoke out against abortion.

— 9 —

I ended up working at the lodge after my first year at my new school, and I found that I was a pretty good waitress. All those years of hiding how I felt and showing the world a happy face came in handy when serving grumpy customers. I enjoyed my work there, and after a while, my duties were extended. I worked there nearly every summer through high school. My second year there I also cooked, ran the cash register, and helped to clean the cabins for new guests.

My third and last year at the lodge brought both blessing and cursing. It was my favorite year because I was finally allowed a position as a horse wrangler and guide. I had spent enough time with the horses the previous two years that my boss deemed me competent and allowed me the job when I asked. I loved working with the horses and having the chance to ride into the woods on a regular basis.

Even so, it was the worst year because I was sexually assaulted by the head cook, who was old enough to be my father. Have you ever woken from a night terror, covered in sweat and trembling, only to slip back into its heavy handed grasp? The nightmare had returned, and so vividly, that I didn't know what to do. Once again, I was afraid to tell anyone. But I told my mom anyway, and once again, she believed me. She and my father went back to the lodge to report the incident to my boss.

After the head cook was fired, I could have gone back. I would have been safe. Still, I was afraid. With the assault still fresh in my mind, I was scared that my memories would try to overcome me once again. Instead, I spent the next summer driving a tractor for my uncle's haying business. It didn't pay much, but it got me away from the world for a while. He lived in Colorado, and I went to stay with him for a couple of months while I worked.

My senior year, Josey started preschool. She had grown to be such a smart little girl! I remember how proud I was when her teacher informed us that she had been dubbed the official puzzle queen by her class. Although I was probably a bit biased, I thought that her artwork was far better than what the other kids made, and she did much better academically.

I was blessed to have the opportunity to spend some time in my daughter's class with her. Because of my diligence in school, I had only a minimum of classes that I needed to complete that year. This enabled me to sit in on several of Josey's school days before I needed to start my own. I loved watching her learn. She was a little shy with the other kids at first, but once she opened up she was a little spitfire!

I chuckle at the memory of Josey trying to tell everyone that she had two moms. Thankfully, most everyone knew the situation already and understood what she was saying. We never hid the truth from Josey. However, children learn to address people as others address them. My siblings and I called my mom "Mom," so that's what she learned. Everyone called me "Anna," so that's what she usually called me. While part of me wished that she would call me "Mom," I understood why she didn't. Like so much of my life, this was unique and bittersweet.

Like most people of that age, life hit me hard my senior year. It sunk in that I needed to figure out what I was doing for the rest of my life. I thought about attending college but didn't know exactly what I wanted to study. I also knew I didn't have the time or the funds to play with the college experience until I figured it out. I knew I needed reliable work so I would be able to begin supporting myself and Josey full-time. I enjoyed waitressing, but I wanted to be able to do better for her.

I was absent on the day that the army recruitment officer came to my school, but I heard about it the next day. Several of the other students were talking about the idea of enlisting, but few were seriously considering it. For me, however, it seemed like the perfect solution to my problem. I found one of the cards that the recruitment officer had left at the school and called him after I got home. We made arrangements to meet and discuss what I might be able to do.

After meeting with the officer, I was even more certain that this was the right path for me to take. I would have a steady paycheck and benefits, which was something I had never had. As a bonus, I could get job training, and it would even pay for college should I decide to pursue another avenue once I got out. If I did this, Josey and I would be set. There was just one problem—they would not allow me to enlist as a single parent with sole custody of my child.

I went home that night wondering what else I might be able to do. The army had seemed like the perfect solution to my problem, but if they would not allow me to enlist, I would have to find something else. I discussed the situation with my parents, and they helped me to consider my options. After several hours of deliberation, we came up with an idea.

Because I would have had to leave Josey with my mom during my basic training, we decided we could file for joint custody, with my mom acting as Josey's legal guardian. That way, I could go ahead and enlist. Once I had completed my training and was stationed, Josey would come live with me. I called my recruiter the next morning, and he agreed that it should satisfy the legal requirements.

My father called his lawyer and had the paperwork drawn up. Within a matter of days, we were standing before the county judge telling him the reasons for the shared guardianship. He agreed with the need for the request and granted it. A couple weeks later, I traveled to Salt Lake City with my recruiter so I could be tested to see what jobs would be open to me.

I scored well in all the tests and passed both the physical and mental exams. Of the different options, I decided I wanted to become a military police officer. With a little work, I managed to arrange things so that I would be stationed at Fort Bragg once I had completed basic training, which might allow me to earn the opportunity to join the airborne division. Because I still had several months until I graduated, I was placed in the delayed entry program. This meant I would have the opportunity to complete some of the classroom work for my training, but wouldn't actually ship out until the following June after graduation.

By the time I returned home, I was elated. I felt like I was practically walking on air. Finally, I had a plan and had taken the first steps to implement it! I was going to be able to care for my daughter and provide her with the life I believed she deserved. I couldn't wait until my papers arrived so I could get a head start. My recruiter had told me that if I finished all my coursework before I shipped out, I would be able to qualify for promotion nearly immediately.

My senior year seemed to fly by. I would spend most of my weekday mornings working on my army coursework, with a few days helping out in Josey's preschool class. Afterward, I would go to school and then work. I was employed as a waitress at one of the local restaurants at the time. While the pay wasn't the best, it wasn't bad for what my little town had to offer.

I've often wondered what my life would be like now if I had kept my course and continued into the army, but I never made it that far. Instead, I fell in love—or at least, I thought I did.

— 10 —

It was February 2, 2000, the first time I saw him. I remember this because it was his birthday, as well as his first day as a cook at the restaurant where I was waitressing. He was new to town and very good looking. His name was Keith, and he was five years older than me. I was more than a little surprised when he asked me if he could walk me home from work after we cleaned up that night. I had not dated much in school and felt rather awkward around him. Added to my own social ineptness was the knowledge that there was no way this boy would be interested in me if he knew my history.

Even after he found out, though, he remained interested. Our relationship moved quickly, but I didn't care. He took me out to the movies and bought me flowers, chocolates, and a stuffed teddy bear. He would cuddle with me on the couch while we watched movies, and he told me how amazing I was. I could hardly believe that this fabulous, gorgeous guy would be interested in a girl like me, but somehow he was.

A month before I was to graduate, and for the third time in my life, we found out that I was pregnant. I was terrified to tell my parents. I knew how disappointed they would be. I would also have to notify my recruitment officer and let him know that we had a change in plans. When I told Keith, he was thrilled. He told me how much he loved me and asked me to marry him. While it wasn't what I had envisioned for my future, I was happy with the idea. Instead of becoming a soldier, I would become a wife.

I received some strange looks during my last few weeks at school. Once again there were whispers. This time, however, it was because of my choices and my actions. I didn't mind so much this time. I was in love and about to be married. And I was going to have another baby! I was excited for this pregnancy. After all, Josey had survived, so I knew I could do it again. I was much more confident about having this child.

Keith and I were married in early June, just a few weeks after I had graduated. It was a small wedding, with just a few friends and family. It was beautiful, though, and I couldn't have been happier. Keith had already found us a house to move into, and I couldn't wait to start making it into a home. I had been dreaming and planning how I would become the most excellent wife and mother that a family could wish to have.

This was my chance to create that perfect family that I had always desired.

Things went well for the first couple of weeks. My parents agreed to keep Josey at their house while I fixed up the house he had found. I attempted to plant some morning glories near our front porch, and I couldn't wait for them to bloom. I envisioned drinking our morning cup of coffee together on a porch swing and watching the flowers unfold. I did my best to decorate on our meager budget, and I also attempted to learn to cook.

I should have left when I discovered he was an alcoholic. I should have, but I didn't. I was so enthralled with the idea of making everything work that I stayed where I was. I thought that if I just loved him enough, I could change him, and that for once in my life, I could have my dream. However, he usually spent nearly all of his paycheck on either drugs or alcohol, and I knew I was watching my dream wither and die.

There were several times that I packed my few belongings, intending to return home to my parent's house. Each time, however, I lost my courage to do so. I won't write here all the things he did when he caught me trying to leave, but I will say that it was not pleasant. Although my parents suspected abuse, they could do nothing because I would admit nothing. Although she did come to spend the night with me occasionally, we did not allow Josey to move in with us.

At that time, there was a girl who would come over to visit us fairly regularly. I considered her my best friend. We would play video games and talk. For the most part, I stayed home and tried to show my husband what a good wife I could be.

My pregnancy progressed normally, and I was so excited to discover that I would be having a little boy. Keith had wanted a boy, and I thought that the news would please him. Maybe this would help him to settle down and become more responsible and caring; I couldn't wait to give him the news. However, while he was delighted to have a little boy, he did not change.

We found out that there was a difficulty with the pregnancy when I was about six months along. I went into premature labor and had to be rushed to the hospital in Vernal. They kept me there for three days, giving me medications to stop the contractions. My water had not broken, and they needed to make the labor stop so my little boy could stay where he was and keep growing. They told us that I was anemic and malnourished. I tried telling them that I just didn't have an appetite. I didn't want anyone to know that my husband had spent all of our money on his addictions, and that we didn't have the funds remaining to buy groceries.

When I was finally allowed to leave the hospital, they told me that I would need to reduce my stress level and take better care of myself, or I might lose my baby. I was sure that Keith would understand the danger and do everything possible to save his son. Even if he wouldn't straighten up for me, he would do it for the baby. Unbeknownst to me, I was getting ready to encounter more stress than I had experienced in a very long time. Would it ever stop? Was I to endure season after season of suffering, loneliness, and heartache?

When I returned home, my in-laws had us over to their house. My parents joined us as well. My mom had arranged for all of us to be there. She said that she had something that we all needed to hear. I was curious but not overly worried. I was thinking that the meeting would be to discuss something small, like a baby shower, or perhaps what we needed to do as a family to make sure that my little boy would be well. Maybe all the parents were going to talk with Keith about being a better husband and father.

Instead, she forced Keith to admit what he had done while I had been in the hospital fighting for our son's life. The truth came out like a cockroach beneath old furniture, and it was just as ugly. He had been sleeping with my best friend. I was devastated. I had been betrayed by two of the most important people in my life. I was inconsolable. Once again, my world had been turned upside down, and I didn't know what to do.

I was too upset to drive after hearing what he had done, so my mom drove me back to her house. We decided that it would be best if I stayed with them until I knew what I was going to do. I remember that I was lying on my old bed crying when Keith came in. He swore to me that it was a one-time thing, and that he was sorrier than I could imagine. He promised that it would never happen again and that I could trust him.

I wanted so badly to believe him. I knew that if he was lying, then all that I had been working for would be lost. I would never have the family that my heart longed for so deeply. He also promised me that the drinking and the drugs would stop immediately. He would go home and flush everything if I would just take him back.

I said yes. I shouldn't have, but I did.

We walked out to tell my parents what I had decided. My mom started crying. She told me that I couldn't take him back. I needed to tell him to leave and never look back. It surprised me when she said that. I was certain that she would be happy that we were going to work things out, and that he was going to start being a proper husband and father. Why was she so upset?

That was when she told me that she had also discovered that he had tried to molest Josey. Everything started spinning. I couldn't breathe.

Mom helped me to a chair and told me to put my head down and concentrate on breathing. I vaguely remember my mom telling Keith that he either needed to call the police and turn himself in, or she would do it for him. I'm guessing that she must have looked terrifying to him, because he made the call. I was still trying to master the art of inhaling when they arrived to arrest him.

The next several weeks passed in a fog for me. After the doctors had finished inspecting Josey, they told us that he had not managed any penetration, so Keith could only be charged with molestation, not rape. Keith admitted to the authorities what he had done, and he was sentenced to one year in prison. Once he arrived in prison, the authorities there added time to his sentence. While the judge in Manila had said he believed that Keith was truly sorry for what he had done, the state officials saw through his lies and gave him a slightly harsher ruling. He was to serve only five years for hurting my little girl. Five years? One hundred and five years would not come anywhere close to the punishment this beast deserved for what he had done. How could I, knowing what I knew of darkness, look into that sweet face again without that poisonous fear? Without that toxic rage?

Something within me broke; all I could feel was shame. It was my poor choices and bad decisions that had put my little girl in a situation where something like that could happen to her. I went through the motions of surviving over the next several weeks, but I cannot say that I was living. I ate, I slept, and I cried. I hated myself, and the weak creature I had become. I had lost sight of everything because of a boy— a coward—a monster.

At my next appointment with my doctor, we were told that I needed to find a place to stay in Vernal. Manila was too far away from the hospital, and I was not doing well. If my stress level didn't come down rapidly, I could lose my baby. The thought terrified me, but I had no idea what to do about it. Everything had spun out of control. I couldn't change my circumstances, and I didn't know how to change my reactions to them.

It was decided that I would move in with my grandmother for the remainder of my pregnancy. She had a spare room in her apartment and was willing to care for me until my son arrived. It was also thought that a change of scenery would do me some good. I had always enjoyed staying with grandma, and I needed some time away from everyone while I tried to recover from the events of the past few months.

I spent a great deal of time at the library, reverting to using books as a way to escape reality. Grandma was okay with this, as I would at least get some exercise walking back and forth to retrieve and return my books. I ate each meal with my grandmother, and slept a great deal. Little by little, my son's health improved, as did my own. Physically, at least, I was improving.

With the help of my family, my mental condition was recovering at a much slower rate. While I did not yet have the fight in me that had been present with my daughter, I began to look forward to the birth of my little boy.

In what now seems like the space of a single breath, my son arrived. The labor and birth were much easier with him than they had been with Josey. Within hours of being admitted to the hospital, I was holding my little man in my arms. Naming him was slightly more complicated for me than naming my daughter had been. His father had chosen the name Jacob, and although I wanted to erase every memory I had of that time, it was too late. The baby's name had already stuck. I will admit that out of spite, I gave Jake the middle name of "Brian." I was a die-hard Backstreet Boys fan at the time, and Keith absolutely despised them. Giving my son that name was my first act of defiance against what he had done to us. Once again, I was faced with being a young single mother. While the prospect did not thrill me, I had enough experience by then to know that I could do it.

— 11 —

After Jake's birth, I returned home to Manila. I wasn't sure what I needed to do to begin building a future for my little family, but I did know that I needed to return to the workforce. I made that my first priority and decided that for now, even achieving one goal was an improvement. I was still suffering from severe depression and had trouble concentrating on much of anything. Still, I could do nothing to get ahead if I was not employed.

It took a little time for me to find a job, but after a while, I found myself working as a janitor for the high school. It wasn't my favorite job, but I got to work by myself for the most part, and I needed that. I had a lot of time to think while cleaning the classrooms. I began to develop a plan to change my situation. It wasn't much of a plan, but it was all I had.

After working out a few of the details in my mind, I told my parents that I was going to move out. I needed to get back on my feet and act like an adult. I needed to get a better job and a house of my own. After a great deal of deliberation and discussion, it was decided that Josey would stay with my parents. She was accustomed to my mom in the "mother" role, and my new start would be easier if I only had Jake with me. Jake was nearly a year old by that time, and would be a handful by himself.

I made a few phone calls, and a week later I was on my way. I had a little Toyota Tercel at the time. While it only ran about half the time, it would have to suffice until I could afford something better. I loaded up Jake and our few belongings and headed to Colorado. I had family in a little town called Meeker. My older sister allowed me to stay with her for the first few days that I was there.

It didn't take me long to find a job working as a cashier at one of the local gas stations, and it only took me a few days longer to find an apartment for us. I will be the first to admit that it wasn't the most ideal home, but the price was right. The bathroom was minuscule, having only a shower and no bathtub. Jake had to have his baths in the kitchen sink. The kitchen had no cupboards, just a sink, stove and fridge. It had two bedrooms, though, and that was sufficient. My younger sister moved in with me, taking the second bedroom.

We made a deal that I would cover her living expenses if she would babysit Jake for me. I had made plans to take on a second job as a housekeeper at the local hospital, but needed someone I could trust to care for my boy while I worked. I knew that I would never get ahead by working at the gas station. I could survive, but I still wanted more for my kids. I wasn't afraid of work, so work I did.

Monday through Friday, I would work at the hospital during the mornings from 5 AM to 4 PM. Afterward, I would make a quick trip home to check on my son before I had to be at work at the gas station at 4:30. I worked there until around 11:30 PM, when I would go home and pass out. Four days a week I had a half day off, and I worked all day the other three. I worked all weekends and many holidays at the gas station. It wasn't much of a life, but I was standing on my own two feet, and I was proud of that.

The depression I had been experiencing gradually receded as I worked more. I'm not sure if time was slowly healing my heart, or if I was just too busy and exhausted to think about it. Either way, I was recovering day by day. While I missed Josey terribly, I was glad that my parents had convinced me to let her stay with them. I felt that Jake was too young to notice that I wasn't around much, but Josey would have felt abandoned. On the few holidays that I had off from both jobs, I would travel home to see her, and it broke my heart each time I had to leave again. I was always surprised at how completely my fractured heart could still be broken.

Between caring for my family and working, my life was full. I had no interest in starting a relationship with anyone. I was weary of making friends and didn't even want to consider risking my still-tender heart again. If I had my way, I would raise my kids and then spend the rest of my life alone. It would be safer that way for me and for my children. As long as I didn't let anyone close, no one could hurt us.

God, it seems, had other plans for my life.

I met the man who would become my husband just a few days before Jake's first birthday. He had come into the gas station with some friends to buy some snacks. He was bigger than his friends, and seemed to intimidate some of my other customers. For some reason, he didn't scare me. One of his buddies came to the counter first and promptly began flirting with me. I was not impressed.

When he made it to the counter, he introduced himself as Jim, and tried to strike up a conversation. I shut him down nearly as quickly as I had his friend, and they left after paying for their items. He was back the next day, though, and the one after. Each time he came, he would try to start a conversation and then ask me to go on a date with him. Each time, I turned him down.

Finally, after two weeks of this, I made him an offer. He could come over to my house on my next night off. I would invite some of my other friends, and we would play cards for a while. But after that, he had to promise to leave me alone. He agreed. I wasn't really worried about him wanting to see me again after that. I was sure that once he saw how much baggage I came with, he would run the other way and not look back.

During this time, my father had started drinking again. As a result, my parents divorced a second time. Mom had taken Josey and moved to Parachute, Colorado. Parachute was less than an hour drive from Meeker, so I was able to see Josey on most of my days off. It was working well for all of us. I was grateful to have them so close, where I could see my family more frequently, and Josey was happy because she got to see her baby brother. She absolutely adored playing with him. She treated him just like one of her dolls. Mom and I loved watching them, and would spend hours laughing at their antics.

Jim was supposed to come over on the next Friday night. I had managed to get the night off by trading schedules with one of my co-workers. I didn't clean up my house. I didn't get dressed up or put on any makeup. I was tired from working, and I really just wanted to get the whole deal over with so I could keep moving on with my life. My sister agreed to hang around until everyone showed up, but then she had made plans to go out with some of her own friends. I was glad that she would stick around for me, just in case Jim was the first to arrive. And he was.

To say that he impressed my sister would be an understatement. Not long after his arrival, she drug me into the bathroom so she could speak with me privately. She wanted me to ask him if he would be interested in dating her, since I wasn't interested in dating him. I said I would ask, and I did.

He told me that he was only interested in me, not my sister. I was flattered, but I still wasn't interested in starting any kind of relationship. After all, look at what had happened the last time! I had horrible taste in men. I obviously couldn't see past a handsome face, so the best thing for me to do was just stay away from men all together. I just had to convince Jim of that.

I brought my son out to play on a blanket near the table where we would be playing cards. I thought that would send him running, but I had other baggage just in case it didn't. As it turned out, Jim wasn't concerned with Jake at all. He really didn't care that I was a single mom. I was surprised to find that I actually enjoyed his company. He was funny, intelligent, and caring. While we were getting to know each other, I told him about Josey, and he accepted that too. It seemed like nothing would scare this guy away.

At one point that evening, I happened to mention to one of my friends that I would need a ride to work the next Monday because my car had been acting up and I wouldn't have the money to get it into a shop until the next week. I really hated that car. There was something wrong with it, and it never wanted to run when I needed it to. My friend said she could help me out and would be at my place bright and early to pick me up. The rest of the evening passed fairly pleasantly, and before long, it was late enough for me to politely send everyone home. I didn't have work the next morning, and was relishing the idea of sleeping in an extra hour or so.

I actually slept in a little longer than planned. My sister was being nice to me that morning, and kept Jake occupied until almost nine. When I stumbled out to get some coffee, I found that Jim had come back. He was outside, working on my car. He had been there for an hour already, had gone to the parts store, gotten the materials he needed, and was fixing my car for me. I was dumbfounded. The night before I had told him that not only was I not interested in him, but that he really shouldn't be interested in me. Why was he here?

After I had managed to pry my eyelids open and my jaw off the floor, I got dressed and took him a cup of coffee as well. I wanted to know why he was there, and why he was fixing my car. I also wanted to know how much the parts had cost and how much money I owed him for fixing things. I was almost irritated that he didn't take the hint the night before. How many different ways did I need to tell this guy "no" before he understood it?

Jim was grateful for the coffee, but when I asked him how much he wanted, he was surprised. He said that he didn't want anything, and he wasn't going to tell me how much the parts were. He just wanted to help me. I wasn't quite sure how to react to that. He told me that he got the point that I wasn't interested, but he still was, and he had every intention of continuing to try for just as long as he could.

Needless to say, I did eventually give in. I was going to be smart about it this time, though. I was going to have him move in with me so I would know him well before I agreed to marry him. He was also an alcoholic before we got together. After my experiences with my father, I couldn't stand for that. I told him if he wanted to be with me, he would have to stop drinking. He chose wisely. We found out that I was pregnant the spring of 2002. Jim was so excited.

Because of the health issues I had experienced with Jake, it was decided that I would leave the workforce, and Jim would provide for us until after the baby came. Jim found a job that was supposed to pay better near Vernal, so we returned to my old stomping grounds. Jim was a good, hard worker. Unfortunately, his boss wasn't all that great about making sure that his employees were paid. Somehow, though, we managed to get by until our daughter Jasmyne was born.

Jazzy's birth was a terrifying experience. At my last prenatal appointment with her, my doctor told us that she had stopped growing, and something was wrong. He didn't know what it was, but there was a problem with my little girl. It was decided that I would be admitted to the hospital where they would induce labor in an effort to save my baby. I'm not sure if I was more worried or if Jim was. We were willing to do whatever was necessary to save our child.

I don't remember the labor itself lasting for very long after the induction. I do clearly remember the furious look on Jim's face when my daughter was born and the first words out of the doctor's mouth were: "Oh, so that was what was wrong with her." Jazzy's umbilical cord had wrapped around her neck and had knotted in one area, cutting off the oxygen and vital nutrients that she needed for proper growth. We couldn't understand how the doctor had not seen that in the ultrasounds.

Praise be to God, our little girl was healthy. Action had been taken quickly enough that any serious damage had been avoided. She was small, only 4 lb. 8 oz., but she was healthy enough that she was able to come home with us in just a matter of hours. She was eating well and had obviously inherited her father's stubborn streak. Before we left the hospital, the doctor had a warning for me. He felt I should not have any more children, as doing so could have the potential to kill both me and the child.

Jim and I finally married in June 2003. It was a beautiful wedding. Josey was the flower girl and looked absolutely adorable in her dress. She thoroughly enjoyed showing off to everyone in attendance. Jake wasn't impressed with the wedding. He did not like getting dressed up and liked it even less that he was supposed to stand still throughout the service, holding the pillow with the rings. I couldn't stop smiling. It wasn't the biggest wedding or the fanciest. But I was marrying the greatest man on the planet, and I couldn't wait.

Within a year, we discovered that Jazzy had problems that had not been detected at her birth. By the time she was eight months old, she had begun having fevers that came once every month. Her temperature would soar to 103–104°F, and stay there for three or four days. Nothing we did could bring the temperatures down. We took her to countless doctors, trying to diagnose the problem, but no one could give an explanation. Even pediatric specialists were unable to discover what was wrong with her.

Finding out I was pregnant for the fourth time could not have come at a worse time for us. Jim was working for my father, cutting timber in the mountains outside Manila. I was waitressing again. We had little money, and nearly all that we had was going towards Jazzy's hospital bills. We had hit the time of month for her fevers to start up again, and had taken her back to the hospital in Vernal for more testing. The doctors there had decided it would be necessary to do a diagnostic spinal tap.

I had not been feeling well for several days, and, with a knowing suspicion, had bought a pregnancy test. While Jim sat outside Jazzy's room, I went and took the test. It was positive. We were going to have another baby. Sitting in that hospital bathroom, I cried. I had no idea how we were going to handle another child. We were barely scraping by as it was. Our hands were full with our other children, not to mention the warning given by the doctor after Jazzy had been born.

Feeling defeated, I went and told Jim. He put his arm around me and told me it would be alright. He would take care of us, and he did. He decided that it wasn't good for us to be around my father's alcoholism, and moved us back to Colorado. We moved to Parachute so I could be closer to Josey and my mom. I loved being closer to them. I could easily walk down the street to visit, and did so regularly.

The doctors never did figure out what was causing Jazzy's fevers. We just learned how to do the best we could to keep her cool and comfortable until they passed. We were told there was a chance that she would simply grow out of them. We hoped so, but were left without any options for helping our little girl.

As with my other children, the pregnancy for my youngest child advanced fairly uneventfully until the very end. We found out that we were going to have a little boy. Josey wanted to name him Aladdin because her sister had been named Jasmyne. She was tickled with the idea, but Jim and I decided to name him Tanner instead. While she was crushed that she wouldn't have any more Disney characters running around the house, Josey was still excited to have another baby brother to play with.

Jim had found a good job at a welding shop just a couple towns over. Financially, we were nearly stable once again. Jim had even found the means to buy us a new car, so I would have something reliable to drive the kids around in. Life was looking up, and I was beginning to anticipate the arrival of our little boy. The problems that seemed so huge at the beginning of my pregnancy had either passed, or we had found better ways to deal with them.

I went into labor on the night of February 3, 2004. Tanner was a little early, but this was not a cause for concern. All the other kids were excited to meet their little brother, and Jim and I were both excited to meet our newest little guy as well. At the hospital, the doctor was concerned because Tanner was not facing the right direction. He had turned sideways, and his left elbow was in the position where his head should have been. They had to try to turn him, the doctor said, or there would be a serious risk to the two of us. Trying to turn my baby from the outside was painful, but we didn't have much choice. Unfortunately, it didn't work. Tanner refused to budge.

The doctor told us that Tanner would have to be born via cesarean section. The doctor decided that due to my medical history with pregnancies, he wanted to perform a tubal ligation while they had me open. I already had four children, and the problems seemed to be getting worse with each one. The doctor believed it was the best course of action for my health.

I wish that I could have consulted another medical professional about this, as I have since learned that their advice may have been erroneous. However, at the time I did not have any other information and agreed to have the procedure.

I didn't mind the sight of blood. The human body had always been fascinating to me. I had even worked as an emergency medical technician not long after Jake was born, and I had loved it. The surgery itself didn't bother me. I did find it comical, however, when I saw Jim's face go green as they cut me open. My husband has been a hunter all his life, and had worked on a farm for years as a teen. He was no stranger to the sight of blood. He just couldn't handle it when it was my blood that he was seeing. Still, he stayed with me through the entire process.

For the first time, my baby was able to go home before I was. They allowed him to stay with me, but he was healthy and ready to go home right away. Because of the surgery, I had to stay in the hospital for a few days. Jim and my mom took turns bringing my kids out to see the baby and me. I enjoyed having all of them visit and watching my kids all playing and interacting with each other. I was so proud of each of them.

Several months after Tanner was born, Jim transferred to another job in a town near Meeker, so we moved again. He was working on a pipeline, which paid better, but required that he put in a great deal more time. Frequently, he would go two or three days before he was able to come home. It was hard on our family, but we had decided that we wanted to start the process of buying a home rather than moving and renting different homes all the time. We wanted something permanent, and that took money.

After a while, we decided that his work at the pipeline just wasn't going to work for us. He found yet another job close to Meeker. It only paid slightly less but still required a lot of hours. But at least he was home every night. I also took a job waitressing, while a friend would watch our children. While we were getting by pretty efficiently, it wasn't the lifestyle that we wanted for our family. We had enough money to do pretty much whatever we wanted to do, but we didn't get to spend enough time together.

After a serious talk about what we wanted for our family and what we wanted for our future, we made some pretty big changes. We knew we could continue saving for a home, but we would be missing some of the most important parts of our kids' lives. Instead, we decided to head north to Montana. Jim did some searching online and found a job that had advancement opportunities in Kalispell. After they accepted his application, it was decided that he would go ahead of us and find a place to rent. Because the starting wage at his new job was pretty low, we would have to use our savings to cover our expenses while he worked his way up to better pay.

I AM THE EXCEPTION

After Jim left, I gave my notice at work and began packing. It didn't take him long to find us a house. I was very pleased to find that our new home was to be a log cabin just off a small lake. It was beautiful, and I loved my new home. It didn't take us long to unpack and get settled in. We quickly developed a routine. Jim and I would get up early in the mornings so he could go to work. After he left, I would wake the children and bathe them, and then we would explore the area around our home. It was a nice life. I wondered if this was what "normal" felt like?

I missed Josey, though. Because of her schooling and other considerations, she had stayed in Colorado with my mom. Jim and I did our best to make sure that we visited for the holidays, but were sometimes detained due to the Montana's fierce winters. After a while, I did acquire a computer and was able to keep in touch via the Internet.

I was lonely. Even though I had my three small children with me all day, Jim was gone to work most of the time. I knew no one in our area, and didn't really know how to go about making friends. For the most part, I retreated back into my books. I didn't know what else to do. I couldn't really see much purpose in my daily life. My eyes had yet to be opened to what was right in front of me.

— 12 —

We had arrived in Montana during the last part of October 2004. It wasn't until February of the following year that I really started having any contact with our new neighbors. We lived a fair distance out of town, and many of our neighbors were only summertime residents. Of the few that stayed year round, many didn't even know that we were there, as my husband had our only vehicle with him when he went to work each day.

Once they did know that we were there, however, I began to receive visitors every now and then. One neighbor in particular stood out from the others—we'll call her Becky. She was different. She had a peace about her that I just couldn't understand. Regardless of what was going on in her life, she had a constant joy that I envied. I didn't know what she had, but I would have given anything to have it too.

As we got to know each other better, she asked me if I knew Christ. I told her that I knew of Him but didn't really have much use for the Bible or religion. She then challenged me to join her in a Bible study. I didn't really care to learn more about God. After all, I had already experienced His form of "love" and didn't care for it. However, I was interested in finding out more about what made this woman "tick," and I was very interested in spending more time with other adults while my husband was at work. So, I accepted her invitation.

A few days later, I went into town with Jim so I could buy myself a cheap Bible. It was the first one I had touched since I was a child. I will admit to feeling a little trepidation about reading the book. I had hated God for so long that I did not want to have anything to do with Him, including reading His Word. However, my desire to find out what had given my new friend that mysterious peace overruled my distaste for religion.

When we got home, I placed the book on the shelf until the day that Becky had agreed to come over to start the study. I hadn't even opened the thing. I noticed it, though, every time I walked past it. It unsettled something in me, though I couldn't decide what. I wasn't sure if I wanted to read it or throw it out of the house. I chalked it up to me just being silly, and left it there until our study day.

When the day finally came, I was surprisingly anxious for her arrival. I had thought of little else for the past several days. I knew that she was going to try to convince me to give my life to God. I was determined to show her that either God was not real, or that He wasn't who she thought He was. After all, how could she reconcile what had happened to me with a just and loving God? In my mind, there was just no way that the two could exist simultaneously.

Before we began, she prayed. She prayed that my heart would be softened and my eyes opened. She prayed that He would show me His love and His constant presence. She prayed that He would reveal Himself and His truth to me through His written word.

She prayed, and He answered.

Over the course of the next several weeks, I became a student once again. Together we read through the books of John, Romans and the Psalms. On my own, I studied the other Gospels, Acts and various parts of the Old Testament. The more I read, the more I wanted to read. The more I learned, the more questions I had. Becky was never bothered by my questions, though. She always answered them willingly.

I would go to bed at night, and verses that I had read throughout the day would run through my mind. There was a lot of what I was learning that I didn't like. I didn't like thinking that I was a sinner. After all, I personally knew several people who were much worse than me. I did like that I could be saved from my sin; I did not like that anyone could. If anyone could be forgiven, then my former stepfather and my ex-husband could be forgiven.

I was still so angry and so full of hate that this thought was unbearable to me. How could they be forgiven?! Couldn't God see what they had done? Shouldn't they be punished for the hurt that they had caused? How was that fair? How was that just?

I asked Becky these questions, and the verses she showed me rocked my world. They completely shook the foundation of everything that I believed.

She took me once again to the book of Romans, and first showed me verses 3:9–10. Here it told me that there is no one who is righteous. Not a single person. All of us have sinned and fallen short of the glory of God. That meant that any sin, even the smallest lie, was enough to separate me from God. God was so just and so holy that sin of any kind could have no home with Him. Here, I had to admit that I was indeed a sinner. I could not deny it.

She then showed me Romans 6:23. It said that all sin causes death, but eternal life can be found in Jesus Christ. That meant that without the saving power of the blood of Christ, I was headed straight for Hell, just like my former stepfather and my ex-husband. We were no different. All of us had sinned and all of us needed to trust in Christ to be saved.

Then came the really hard part. *She told me I had to forgive them.*

I wasn't ready to do that just yet. I wanted to hold on to my anger. It was so much a part of me at that time that I didn't know what I would do without it. I was like a drug addict who knew that the drugs were killing me, but I hung on to them anyway because the withdrawals hurt too much.

Around that same time, we found out that my former stepfather had been released from prison. I started having flashbacks and nightmares again. I would wake up in a cold sweat, feeling like I had run a marathon. At one point, the nightmare was so real that my husband had to pin me down in bed to keep me from hurting myself or him.

Jim took me out a couple of days later and taught me how to efficiently use our 12-gauge shotgun, just in case. It helped some, knowing that I could defend myself and my family if necessary. But it still didn't completely take away the fear, and did nothing to touch the pain.

Something was changing in me, though. I could feel something shifting. While I still wasn't ready to become one of those "Jesus freaks," I was starting to see that maybe God wasn't the uncaring Creator that I had believed Him to be. I continued with my weekly Bible studies and my private reading. Each day I came closer and closer to the truth. A few weeks later, I stumbled across the verse that changed everything for me.

Jim was at work, and I had just laid the kids down for a nap. The house was quiet, and I had a full cup of coffee sitting in front of me at the table. I was relishing the peace. I started leafing through the pages of my Bible, and I asked God to show me something, anything that would help me to understand. I stopped in the book of Romans.

"And we know that God causes all things to work together for good to those who love God, to those who are called according to His purpose" (Romans 8:28).

The Holy Spirit spoke to my heart, and everything fell into place. I had another flashback, only this one was different. This time I saw how every one of the trials I had endured had brought me to this place, had made me this person. I could see how God had used all those things to make good in my life. For the first time, I could see that He was there! He had been with me the entire time! Now, knowing how His presence tasted, and feeling it in my fingertips, I wondered how I had missed it before.

I was glad there was no one around to see me, because I began to cry. Just a little at first, but before long I was sobbing. How could I have been so blind? There had not been a single trial in which God had not provided for me. Two of my most precious gifts came as a direct result of those horrors, and I would gladly have endured the same again for them. When I had needs, they had always been met. When I was alone, he sent me those who would truly care. He had loved me, and in return I had hated Him. He provided for me, and I cursed Him. He gave me mercy, and I gave him nothing. He drew me close, and I pushed him away. *He died for me, and I effectively spit on his bloodied body.*

I was so ashamed. Instead of seeing all the ways that He had abandoned me, I could now see all the ways that I had rejected Him. I had sinned against Him, repeatedly and intentionally. I had lied, and I had stolen. I had indeed done worse than my rapists. While they had only injured me, I not only wished them dead, but I rejected the One who had died. I was no better. I, too, deserved Hell.

Sitting there at that table, I begged God to forgive me. I told Him that I was so very sorry for all that I had done. I knew the truth now. I wanted to live for Him for whatever time He allowed me to have. And He did forgive me. Even after all I had done to sin against Him, He still loved me enough to forgive me.

I sat there in communion with my Savior for a while longer before I could control myself enough to stand. I couldn't wait to tell my neighbor and my family about what Jesus had done for me. I called my neighbor first, as I knew she would be home. I think she was nearly as excited as I was!

Then I called my mom. I couldn't wait to tell her and Josey! Boy was I in for a surprise, though! She told me that they had recently started attending church themselves, and God had been drawing them in as well! I was in awe of what God had been doing in my family. I cried more tears that day than I had in a very, very long time.

I was baptized in the lake by our house in late October 2005. The water was freezing, but I didn't care. I wanted the world to know that I was now a child of God. My dear neighbor bought me my first study Bible. It became my most treasured possession, and I couldn't wait to dig in. That first year, I think I read through the entire thing twice. After all God had done for me, I couldn't wait to learn more about Him and how He wanted me to live.

Not long after that we had to move again; we needed to be closer to town for Jim's work. The price of gas was just getting to be too much for us to handle. One of our other neighbors had a small cabin just outside town. It was off-grid and didn't have running water, but he would let us stay there rent-free if we would just take care of the property for him.

Our time at the cabin was definitely a learning experience. It felt as though I had been thrown back in time. We hauled our water in every week. We grew a garden. I cooked on a wood stove, and did our laundry in an old ringer washing machine. At night, we would sit around the table and read or do other crafts. I loved it.

After the first winter at the cabin, we decided it was time to make some bigger changes. Jim and I talked to our parents, and we all decided that it would be a great idea if they moved onto the property with us. Our landlord was okay with the idea, and I missed Josey terribly. I was missing so much of her life while she was in Colorado, and so were her siblings.

Mom and Josey arrived in Montana that July, a week before her 13th birthday. She was the same age I had been when I had become pregnant with her. In her, I could see the child that I might have been. I was amazed at how much she had grown and matured since the last time I had seen her. I cried when I saw her, partly because I was so happy that they were there, and partly because I had missed so much of my beautiful daughter's life. I was simply amazed at the person she was becoming.

That night, I went to bed filled with regrets. I wasn't sure what else I could have done for her. My mom and her new husband, Chris, had done a wonderful job raising her while I wasn't there. Still, I wasn't there. Would she understand why? Would she be able to see that I had always done the best I could for her?

I didn't know the answer to these questions. But I did know that she was there, at that time, and I would do my best to show her how much I loved her. I could do nothing to change the past, but with God's help, I could move forward with all my children. I wanted nothing more than to love my family and help them grow up knowing the love of Jesus.

I had been attending a small church not far from our house, and my mom and Josey soon joined me there. Soon Josey and I were volunteering on a regular basis. I sang with the worship team, and Josey ran the projector. We both helped with the children's ministry. I was humbled by her servant's heart and loved watching her with the youngest of the children. They flocked around her every chance they had.

The two of us also volunteered each summer at the church's Vacation Bible School program. I typically taught the arts and crafts class while Josey assisted with the music and dance programs. She also went out each morning to help with the sports and recreation groups. She was loved by not only the other volunteers, but also the other kids. She was the favorite of many.

Because we had decided to homeschool all the kids, we were able to watch as each of them learned new concepts and ideas. Josey excelled in her writing and art classes. Like me, she had developed a love for reading. We frequently found her stealing off into the woods with a book so she could have some quiet while she lost herself in another adventure.

One of the greatest advantages of our simple lifestyle was the time it allowed us to grow closer together as a family. We spent a great deal of our time in the summer in the mountains, picking berries or swimming in one of the many lakes in our area. During the winter, the kids had school, but we also had a great deal of play time. One of the kids' favorite things to do was build snow forts. Living in Montana, we typically have an excess of snow. After the forts had been built, the snowball wars were on!

We spent about two years at that cabin. I remember it as two of the best years of my life. However, Jim and I noticed something that the kids were missing. Aside from our small church, they didn't have a great deal of interaction with other kids. Josey was becoming a beautiful young lady, but didn't really know how to interact socially.

After a long family discussion about the situation, we decided it was time to move into town. We would continue to homeschool, but we wanted our kids to see more of the world. We prayed that what we had taught them during our time at the cabin would be enough to ground them firmly when they were faced with difficult situations.

During our last year at our little church, we attended a "Sanctity of Life" service. That was the first time I had heard about the abortion crisis. The woman who was speaking gave some general facts about what was going on and asked that we all vote pro-life at the next election. I was shocked at what I had heard, and was interested in getting involved. I tried to speak with her after the service to see if there were any other ways that I could help, but was unable to do so.

I did not hear much about abortion after that, and it slid into the back of my mind. I didn't completely forget, but it didn't seem as urgent. After all, if it was as bad as she had said it was, wouldn't there have been more of an outcry about it? The world couldn't possibly be sleeping through another holocaust, could it?

Jim and I went ahead with the move, and before long we were living within the city limits. It was hard getting used to all the noise and activity, but we thought we were doing what was best for our kids. We found another church closer to our house. We also found a youth ministry that highly interested Josey, and they allowed her to volunteer there. There were far more kids her age, and we thought it was an excellent opportunity for her. The other kids soon made friends with some of the neighbors, and they loved the fact that there was a community park just down the street from our new home.

— 13 —

Early in 2012, God began working another change in me. I started having flashbacks and nightmares once again. I wasn't sure what had triggered them this time, so I didn't know what to do to stop them. Jim was worried about me and suggested that I talk to my new pastor about my problem. So I called and made an appointment to meet with the pastor and his wife the next day.

I had gone so long without talking about my past that it was hard getting the words out to tell them why I had asked for the meeting. I was only able to do it by the grace of God. My pastor suggested that I talk to another woman in our church who had been through similar circumstances and now counseled other women. I agreed, and he arranged a meeting.

Her name was Diane, and she was wonderful. She knew exactly what was going on, and why I was having trouble again. Simply put, I had not forgiven. I had still been holding on to the bitterness and hatred in my heart. She told me that God would help to release these if I would let Him. I knew right away she was right; I just didn't know how. After giving me several scriptures to read, she gave me a hug and told me all I needed to do was ask.

I struggled all that week. A part of me wanted to hold on to my anger. It had been with me for so long that to remove it would be like gouging out an eye or cutting off a hand. But mostly, I wanted to let it go and move on. So I asked God. I begged and pleaded with Him to help me to forgive those who had hurt me so badly. Finally, He again showed me something new.

Forgiveness is a choice. It doesn't have to be something you feel. Because we are commanded to forgive, we are expected to obey. Even if we don't "feel" like it. The world is wrong when it tells us to follow our hearts. I must not follow my heart. My heart must follow me, and I must follow Christ.

I could not believe the freedom that simple truth offered me. Now, every time the past begins to overtake me once again, I can remind myself that I am a new creation in Christ. The past is dead, and has no control over me today. While I can never forget, I can choose to forgive.

Later that summer, Jim and I decided it was time to get a computer and have internet access for our home. Josey was approaching her senior year in school, and we would need it for her education. It would also be nice to have so I could communicate with my siblings who were still in Colorado. We had always been reluctant about allowing television or the Internet into our home, as we knew how soaked in worldliness they had become.

It was then that I discovered Facebook. I loved that I could easily see what was going on in my family's lives. I could see pictures of my nieces and nephews and reconnect with some old friends. I searched for Courtney and Alisa, hoping to find them and thank them for being the best friends I had ever had, but was unable to find them. I kept hoping that one day I would be able to tell them how much their friendship had meant to me.

In October of that year, God began working another change into my life. The day started normally enough. I got up, had breakfast with the family, and started the kids on their schoolwork. As had become habit after the kids were working on their assignments, I logged onto Facebook to see how everyone was doing. As I scrolled through my news feed, something caught my eye.

My older sister, Kenda, had shared a graphic that shocked and amazed me. It showed two ultrasound photos of babies, and was captioned "Which of these children was conceived in rape, and which one has the right to live?" Underneath, it simply said "Abolish Human Abortion." I stared at that graphic for several minutes while the words sank into my mind. I remembered what the woman from that Sanctity of Life Sunday had said about abortion, and my confusion as to why there was no outcry if it were really so bad.

I clicked on the link. I wanted to see who had put out this graphic and why. It took me to a page with the title of Abolish Human Abortion. They claimed to be following the commandments of Christ to love their neighbor as themselves, and rescue those who were being led away to slaughter. I could appreciate that. I moved down the page until I found the graphic that originally caught my eye. As I scrolled through the comments, I could not believe the horrible things that people were saying about children conceived in rape, and the women who had them!

I looked across the table and saw my beautiful daughter sitting there quietly reading her history book. Looking back at my computer screen, I saw red. What had my daughter or I done to deserve such treatment? They didn't know her or me! They hadn't been there, so how dare they pretend that they could speak for us?!

I don't even remember now what I wrote. My fingers took over before I could think through what I wanted to say. I just knew that what they were saying was so wrong, and I could not sit there and read their words without responding. Not long after, I received a message from one of the administrators of the page, asking me if I would be willing to write out my testimony so they could share it with others. I told Josey what had happened, and asked her if it would be alright with her if I told our story. She told me to go for it. I spent the rest of that day trying to write a very simplified version of what you have read here.

Once it was finished, I sent my testimony to the administrator to share. The reaction to that short testimony absolutely astounded me. Because of the comments I had read on that initial graphic, I knew there were several misconceptions about rape conception, but I had no idea that so few women like me had spoken out. I could not believe that my story was so rare. Even today, I refuse to believe it. What happened to me is so horrifyingly common in today's world that I know I'm not the only one with a story like this.

That is why I have written this book. Perhaps you are someone like me, who has simply not had the opportunity to speak out yet. If so, don't wait. There are other women and children out there who need to hear us. Those who advocate for our children's death have taken our pain and suffering and are using it to justify the slaughter of millions of innocent children. Please, let your voice be heard!

Perhaps you know someone in a situation similar to mine. I pray God will use the words in this book to show you how you can help her. Love her, support her, and help her to be strong. Show her that she can become a victor instead of a victim.

Please do not push her toward killing her child. It will haunt her for the rest of her life.

If you are currently in a position such as I was in, I would love nothing more than to be able to help you. Please contact one of the groups listed at the end of this book, and we will do whatever we can to get you the help you need. You can do this. You are not alone.

I'm not anyone special. I possess no special abilities or attributes. God will provide to anyone in need. If I can live through what I have faced and overcome each trial, so can anyone else through the power of God.

Promote redemption, not destruction.

If You Need Help

If you find yourself in a situation similar to the author, or in a pregnancy crisis of any kind, please contact the Hand of Hope Pregnancy Help Hotline at (855)-310-HOPE. There are abolitionists in more than 70 cities around the world who are willing to help you however they can. They can also be contacted through `handofhopecommunity.org` and `abolishumanabortion.com`.

If you are a victim of rape and have become pregnant, Choices 4 Life can also provide help and support. They can be contacted through `choices4life.org`.

Made in the USA
Las Vegas, NV
16 September 2021